the
prophets

THE
NEW INTERNATIONAL READER'S VERSION
BOOKS OF THE BIBLE
for kids

NIrV, The Books of the Bible for Kids: The Prophets
Copyright © 2017 by Biblica
Illustrations © 2017 by Zondervan

The Holy Bible, New International Reader's Version®
Copyright © 1995, 1996, 1998, 2014 by Biblica, Inc.®
All rights reserved

Published by Zonderkidz
3900 Sparks Dr. SE, Grand Rapids, Michigan 49546, U.S.A.

www.zonderkidz.com

Library of Congress Catalog Card Number 2017941835

Contents

introduction to The Prophets

The Prophets is a collection of books written many years ago. The Prophets is part of a much bigger collection known as "the Bible."

Long ago God created the world. Everything he made was good. But creation turned its back on God. Suddenly, the whole world was caught up in sin and death.

So God set out to rescue his good creation—to save us from sin and death. He promised a man named Abraham that his family would bring blessing to all nations and make things right.

Years later, God made a covenant, a very serious agreement, with Abraham's grandchildren's grandchildren. This agreement made these people a "kingdom of priests" and a "holy nation" for God. It taught them how to live well. They would help the world know and obey God. The covenant had promises called blessings for the nation if they obeyed God. It also promised curses if they disobeyed.

Sadly, most of the time the nation of Israel lived like the rest of the world, caught up in sin and death. And because one king disobeyed so badly, Israel split into two nations, Israel and Judah.

The prophets spoke for God. They reminded these two nations about their agreement with him. The prophets begged the people to ask for forgiveness and to agree with God that they were wrong. They begged them to start living how God asked them to. The prophets also talked about what would happen to the nations around Judah. They did this because God cares about all nations and wants the whole world to live well.

As you read the prophets, you will see a lot of sad things like hunger, sickness, enemies attacking, and death. These are the curses that the agreement talked about. But the prophets always looked forward to the blessing of God when the people admitted they were wrong.

You will also see a special promise. God promised that someone would come to his people and give them new hearts. Then they could live the way God asked them to without following lists of rules. They would be made new from the inside!

JONAH

introduction to Jonah

God called the prophet Jonah to tell the people of Nineveh that they would be punished soon for how they lived and treated other people. Nineveh was the capital city of the brutal Assyrian Empire. Jonah would rather do anything than ask them to admit their wrongdoing, since he and everyone else hated the Assyrians. He wanted God to judge them, say that they were wrong, and destroy them!

See what happens when Jonah speaks to the people of Nineveh. What does this book tell us about how God feels about people who disobey him?

⟳⟲

A message from the LORD came to Jonah, the son of Amittai. The LORD said, "Go to the great city of Nineveh. Preach against it. The sins of its people have come to my attention."

But Jonah ran away from the LORD. He headed for Tarshish. So he went down to the port of Joppa. There he found a ship that was going to Tarshish. He paid the fare and went on board. Then he sailed for Tarshish. He was running away from the LORD.

But the LORD sent a strong wind over the Mediterranean Sea. A wild storm came up. It was so wild that the ship was in danger of breaking apart. All the sailors were afraid. Each one cried out to his own god for help. They threw the ship's contents into the sea. They were trying to make the ship lighter.

But Jonah had gone below deck. There he lay down and fell into a deep sleep. The captain went down to him and said, "How can you sleep? Get up and call out to your god for help! Maybe he'll pay attention to what's happening to us. Then we won't die."

Here is what the sailors said to one another. "Someone is to blame for getting us into all this trouble. Come. Let's cast lots to find out who it is." So they did. And Jonah was picked. They asked him, "What terrible thing have you done to bring all this trouble on us? Tell us. What do you do for a living? Where do you come from? What is your country? What people do you belong to?"

He answered, "I'm a Hebrew. I worship the LORD. He is the God of heaven. He made the sea and the dry land."

They found out he was running away from the LORD. That's because he had told them. Then they became terrified. So they asked him, "How could you do a thing like that?"

The sea was getting rougher and rougher. So they asked him, "What should we do to you to make the sea calm down?"

"Pick me up and throw me into the sea," he replied. "Then it will become calm. I know it's my fault that this terrible storm has come on you."

But the men didn't do what he said. Instead, they did their best to row back to land. But they couldn't. The sea got even rougher than before. Then they cried out to the LORD. They prayed, "Please, LORD, don't let us die for taking this man's life. After all, he might not be guilty of doing anything wrong. So don't hold us responsible for killing him. LORD, you always do what you want to." Then they took Jonah and threw him overboard. And the stormy sea became calm. The men saw what had happened. Then they began to have great respect for the LORD. They offered a sacrifice to him. And they made promises to him.

⟳𝒜𝒪⟲

Now the LORD sent a huge fish to swallow Jonah. And Jonah was in the belly of the fish for three days and three nights.From inside the fish Jonah prayed to the LORD his God. He said,

"When I was in trouble, I called out to the LORD.
    And he answered me.

When I was deep in the place of the dead,
  I called out for help.
  And you listened to my cry.
You threw me deep into the Mediterranean Sea.
  I was deep down in its waters.
  They were all around me.
All your rolling waves
  were sweeping over me.
I said, 'I have been driven away from you.
  But I will look again
  toward your holy temple in Jerusalem.'
I had almost drowned in the waves.
  The deep waters were all around me.
  Seaweed was wrapped around my head.
I sank down to the bottom of the mountains.
  I thought I had died
  and gone down into the grave forever.
But you are the LORD my God.
You brought my life up
  from the very edge of the pit of death.

"When my life was nearly over,
  I remembered you, LORD.
My prayer rose up to you.
  It reached you in your holy temple in heaven.

"Some people worship the worthless statues of
    their gods.
  They turn away from God's love for them.
But I will sacrifice a thank offering to you.
  And I will shout with thankful praise.
I will do what I have promised.
  I will say, 'LORD, you are the one who saves.'"

The LORD gave the fish a command. And it spit Jonah up onto
dry land.

A message from the LORD came to Jonah a second time. The LORD said, "Go to the great city of Nineveh. Announce to its people the message I give you."

Jonah obeyed the LORD. He went to Nineveh. It was a very large city. In fact, it took about three days to go through it. Jonah began by going one whole day into the city. As he went, he announced, "In 40 days Nineveh will be destroyed." The people of Nineveh believed God's warning. So they decided not to eat any food for a while. And all of them put on the rough clothing people wear when they're sad. That's what everyone did, from the least important of them to the most important.

Jonah's warning reached the king of Nineveh. He got up from his throne. He took off his royal robes. He also dressed himself in the clothing of sadness. And then he sat down in the dust. Here is the message he sent out to the people of Nineveh.

"I and my nobles give this order.

Don't let people or animals taste anything. That includes your herds and flocks. People and animals must not eat or drink anything. Let people and animals alike be covered with the clothing of sadness. All of you must call out to God with all your hearts. Stop doing what is evil. Don't harm others. Who knows? God might take pity on us. He might not be angry with us anymore. Then we won't die."

God saw what they did. He saw that they stopped doing what was evil. So he took pity on them. He didn't destroy them as he had said he would.

But to Jonah this seemed very wrong. He became angry. He prayed to the LORD. Here is what Jonah said to him. "LORD, isn't this exactly what I thought would happen when I was still at home? That is what I tried to prevent by running away to Tarshish. I knew that you are gracious. You are tender and kind. You are slow to get angry. You are full of love. You are a God who takes pity on people.

You don't want to destroy them. Lord, take away my life. I'd rather die than live."

But the Lord replied, "Is it right for you to be angry?"

Jonah had left the city. He had sat down at a place east of it. There he put some branches over his head. He sat in their shade. He waited to see what would happen to the city. Then the Lord God sent a leafy plant and made it grow up over Jonah. It gave him more shade for his head. It made him more comfortable. Jonah was very happy he had the leafy plant. But before sunrise the next day, God sent a worm. It chewed the plant so much that it dried up. When the sun rose, God sent a burning east wind. The sun beat down on Jonah's head. It made him very weak. He wanted to die. So he said, "I'd rather die than live."

But God spoke to Jonah. God said, "Is it right for you to be angry about the plant?"

"It is," Jonah said. "In fact, I'm so angry I wish I were dead."

But the Lord said, "You have been concerned about this plant. But you did not take care of it. You did not make it grow. It grew up in one night and died the next. And shouldn't I show concern for the great city of Nineveh? It has more than 120,000 people. They can't tell right from wrong. Nineveh also has a lot of animals."

remember what you read

1. What is something you noticed for the first time?

_____

_____

_____

_____

2. What questions did you have?

_____

_____

_____

_____

3. Was there anything that bothered you?

_____

_____

_____

_____

4. What did you learn about loving God?

_____

_____

_____

_____

5. What did you learn about loving others?

_____

_____

_____

_____

introduction to Amos

The kingdom of Israel had a lot of money, and they were safe from any enemies. But God was not happy with them because they were disobeying the laws that created the nation. The rich and powerful people were getting even richer by taking money from poor people.

Amos was a shepherd from the southern kingdom of Judah. God told Amos to tell the king and the people of Israel to say they were sorry and live the way God wanted them to. See how he talked about God's punishment of the nations all around Israel. Then he closed the circle around Israel and finally said, "Israel, you're the worst of all of them!" The leaders of Israel were very angry and told Amos to stop. They kicked him out of Israel.

What does Amos teach us about God and his justice, which is when he makes sure people live how he commands them to in his covenant laws?

These are the words of Amos. Here is the vision he saw concerning Israel. Jeroboam, the son of Jehoash, was king of Israel.

He said,

"The LORD roars like a lion from Jerusalem.
　His voice sounds like thunder from Zion.
The grasslands of the shepherds turn brown.
　The top of Mount Carmel dries up."

The LORD says,

"The people of Tyre have sinned again and again.
    So I will judge them.
They captured whole communities.
    They sold them to Edom.
They did not honor the treaty
    of friendship they had made.
So I will send fire to destroy the walls of Tyre.
    It will burn up its forts."

The LORD says,

"The people of Edom have sinned again and again.
    So I will judge them.
They chased Israel with swords
    that were ready to strike them down.
    They killed the women of the land.
They were angry all the time.
    Their anger was like a fire that blazed out.
    It could not be stopped.
So I will send fire to destroy the city of Teman.
    It will burn up Bozrah's forts."

The LORD says,

"The people of Judah have sinned again and again.
    So I will judge them.
They have refused to obey my law.
    They have not kept my rules.
Other gods have led them astray.
    Their people of long ago
    worshiped those gods.
So I will send fire to destroy Judah.
    It will burn up Jerusalem's forts."

The LORD says,

"The people of Israel have sinned again and again.
    So I will judge them.

They sell into slavery those who have done no wrong.
  They trade needy people
  for a mere pair of sandals.
They grind the heads of the poor
  into the dust of the ground.
  They refuse to be fair to those who are crushed.

"A cart that is loaded with grain
  crushes anything it runs over.
  In the same way, I will crush you.
Your fastest runners will not escape.
  The strongest people will not get away.
Even soldiers will not be able
  to save their own lives.
Men who are armed with bows will lose the battle.
  Soldiers who are quick on their feet will not
      escape.
Horsemen will not be able
  to save their own lives.
Even your bravest soldiers
  will run away naked on that day,"
  announces the LORD.

People of Israel, listen to the LORD's message. He has spoken his message against you. He has spoken it against the whole family he brought up out of Egypt. He says,

"Out of all the families on earth
  I have chosen only you.
So I will punish you
  because you have committed so many sins."

The LORD and King never does anything
  without telling his servants the prophets about it.

"I destroyed some of you,
  just as I did Sodom and Gomorrah.

You were like a burning stick that was pulled out of the fire.
  In spite of that, you still have not returned to me,"
  announces the LORD.

"So, people of Israel, I will judge you.
  Because I will do that to you, Israel,
  prepare to meet your God!"

The LORD forms the mountains.
  He creates the wind.
  He makes his thoughts known to human beings.
He turns sunrise into darkness.
  He rules over even the highest places on earth.
  His name is the LORD God Who Rules Over All.

ᘯᘯᘯ

People of Israel, listen to the LORD's message. Hear my song of
sadness about you. I say,

"The people of Israel have fallen.
  They will never get up again.
They are deserted in their own land.
  No one can lift them up."

Here is what the LORD and King says to Israel.

"A thousand soldiers will march out from a city.
  But only a hundred will return.
A hundred soldiers will march out from a town.
  But only ten will come back."

Israel, look to the LORD and live.
  If you don't, he will sweep through
  the tribes of Joseph like a fire.
It will burn everything up.
  And Bethel won't have anyone to put it out.

There are people among you who turn what is fair into
    something bitter.
  They throw down to the ground what is right.

There are people among you who hate anyone who stands
    for justice in court.
    They hate those who tell the truth.

You make poor people pay tax on their straw.
    You also tax their grain.
So, even though you have built stone houses,
    you won't live in them.
You have planted fruitful vineyards.
    But you won't drink the wine they produce.
I know how many crimes you have committed.
    You have sinned far too much.

Among you are people who crush those who have done
    no wrong.
    They accept money from people who want special
    favors.
    They take away the rights of poor people in the courts.
So those who are wise keep quiet in times like these.
    That's because the times are evil.

Look to what is good, not to what is evil.
    Then you will live.
And the Lord God who rules over all
    will be with you,
    just as you say he is.
Hate evil and love good.
    Do what is fair in the courts.
Perhaps the Lord God who rules over all
    will have mercy on you.
After all, you are the only ones left
    in the family line of Joseph.

How terrible it will be for you
    who long for the day of the Lord!
Why do you want it to come?
    That day will be dark, not light.

It will be like a man running away from a lion
  only to meet a bear.
He enters his house and rests his hand on a wall
  only to be bitten by a snake.
The day of the Lord will be dark, not light.
  It will be very black.
There won't be a ray of sunlight anywhere.

The Lord says,

"I hate your holy feasts.
  I can't stand them.
  Your gatherings stink.
You bring me burnt offerings and grain offerings.
  But I will not accept them.
You bring your best friendship offerings.
  But I will not even look at them.
Take the noise of your songs away!
  I will not listen to the music of your harps.
I want you to treat others fairly.
  So let fair treatment roll on
  just as a river does!
Always do what is right.
  Let right living flow along
  like a stream that never runs dry!

∽∾∽

The Lord and King gave me a vision. He was bringing large numbers of locusts on the land. The king's share had already been harvested. Now the later crops were coming up. The locusts stripped the land clean. Then I cried out, "Lord and King, forgive Israel! How can Jacob's people continue? They are such a weak nation!"

So the Lord had pity on them.

"I will let them continue for now," he said.

∽∾∽

Amaziah was priest of Bethel. He sent a message to Jeroboam, the king of Israel. He said, "Amos is making evil plans against you right here in Israel. The people in the land can't stand to listen to what he's saying. Amos is telling them,

" 'Jeroboam will be killed by a sword.
    The people of Israel will be taken away as prisoners.
    They will be carried off from their own land.' "

Then Amaziah said to Amos, "Get out of Israel, you prophet! Go back to the land of Judah. Earn your living there. Do your prophesying there. Don't prophesy here at Bethel anymore. This is where the king worships. The main temple in the kingdom is located here."

Amos answered Amaziah, "I was not a prophet. I wasn't even the son of a prophet. I was a shepherd. I also took care of sycamore-fig trees. But the LORD took me away from taking care of the flock. He said to me, 'Go. Prophesy to my people Israel.' Now then, listen to the LORD's message.

" 'Your land will be measured and divided up.
    And you yourself will die in another country.' "

ᴄᴦᴦᴏ

People of Jacob, you are proud that the LORD is your God. But
        he has made a promise in his own name. He says, "I will
        never forget anything Israel has done.
The LORD and King announces,

"The days are coming
    when I will send hunger through the land.
But people will not be hungry for food.
    They will not be thirsty for water.
Instead, they will be hungry
    to hear a message from me.
People will wander from the Dead Sea to the Mediterranean.
    They will travel from north to east.
They will look for a message from me.
    But they will not find it.

ᘯᙏᙏᖇ

I saw the Lord standing next to the altar in the temple. He said
to me,

"Strike the tops of the temple pillars.
    Then the heavy stones at the base of the entrance will
        shake.
Bring everything down on the heads of everyone there.
    I will kill with my swords
    those who are left alive.
None of the Israelites will escape.
    None will get away.

"You Israelites are just like
    the people of Cush to me,"
    announces the Lord.
"I brought Israel up from Egypt.
    I also brought the Philistines from Crete
    and the Arameans from Kir.

"I am the Lord and King.
    My eyes are watching the sinful kingdom of Israel.
I will wipe it off the face of the earth.
    But I will not totally destroy the people of Jacob,"
    announces the Lord.
"I will give an order.
    I will shake the people of Israel
    among all the nations.
They will be like grain that is shaken through a screen.
    Not a pebble will fall to the ground.
All the sinners among my people
    will be killed by swords.
    They say, 'Nothing bad will ever happen to us.'

ᘯᙏᙏᖇ

"The time will come when I will set up
    David's fallen shelter.

I will repair its broken walls.
  I will rebuild what was destroyed.
  I will make it what it used to be.
Then my people will take control of those
    who are left alive in Edom.
They will also possess all the nations
    that belong to me,"
    announces the LORD.
    He will do all these things.

  I will plant Israel in their own land.
    They will never again be removed
    from the land I have given them,"

says the LORD your God.

remember what you read

1. What is something you noticed for the first time?

_____

_____

_____

_____

2. What questions did you have?

_____

_____

_____

_____

3. Was there anything that bothered you?

_____

_____

_____

_____

4. What did you learn about loving God?

_____

_____

_____

_____

5. What did you learn about loving others?

_____

_____

_____

_____

HOSEA

introduction to Hosea

Israel did not keep the agreement that God made with them when he created their nation. This agreement said the people would love God with all their energy. They would love everyone around them and not hurt them to make their own lives more comfortable. And they would trust only God to protect and provide for them. But God's people provided for themselves by hurting others. They asked other gods to protect them. God was very angry.

God wanted Israel to understand how unfaithful they were. So he told the prophet Hosea to marry Gomer, a woman who would not be faithful to the promise they made when they got married. Hosea was very hurt by Gomer's actions in the same way God wanted Israel to understand that he was very hurt by their actions.

A message from the LORD came to Hosea, the son of Beeri. The message came while Jeroboam was king of Israel. Here is what the LORD said to him.

The LORD began to speak through Hosea. He said to him, "Go. Marry a promiscuous woman. Have children with her. Do this because the people of the land are like that kind of wife. They have not been faithful to me." So Hosea married Gomer. She was the daughter of Diblaim. Gomer became pregnant and had a son by Hosea.

Then the LORD said to Hosea, "Name him Jezreel. That's because I will soon punish Jehu's royal family. He killed many people at the city of Jezreel. So I will put an end to the kingdom of Israel. At that time I will break their military power. It will happen in the Valley of Jezreel."

Gomer became pregnant again. She had a daughter. Then the LORD said to Hosea, "Name her Lo-Ruhamah." Lo-Ruhamah means Not Loved. "That's because I will no longer show love to the people of Israel. I will not forgive them anymore. But I will show love to the people of Judah. And I will save them. I will not use bows or swords or other weapons of war to do it. I will not save them by using horses and horsemen either. Instead, I will use my own power to save them. I am the LORD their God. And I will save them."

Later, Gomer had another son. Then the LORD said, "Name him Lo-Ammi." Lo-Ammi means Not My People. "That's because Israel is no longer my people. And I am no longer their God.

"But the time will come when the people of Israel will be like the sand on the seashore. It can't be measured or counted. Now it is said about them, 'You are not my people.' But at that time they will be called 'children of the living God.' The people of Judah and Israel will come together again. They will appoint one leader and come up out of the land. And Jezreel's day will be great.

"People of Israel, call your brothers 'My people.' And call your sisters 'My loved ones.'

"Tell your mother she is wrong.
    Tell her she is wrong.
She isn't acting like a wife to me anymore.
    She no longer treats me as her husband.
She said, 'I will chase after men who aren't my husband.
    They give me my food and water.
They provide me with wool and linen.
    They give me olive oil and wine.'
She'll look for them.
    But she won't find them.
Then she'll say,
    'I'll go back to my husband.
That's where I was at first.
    I was better off then than I am now.'

She wouldn't admit that I was the one
  who gave her everything she had.
  I provided her with grain, olive oil and fresh wine.
I gave her plenty of silver and gold.
  But she used it to make statues of Baal.

"A new day is coming," announces the LORD.
  "Israel will call me 'my husband.'
  She will no longer call me 'my master.'
She will no longer speak about the gods
  that are named Baal.
  She will not pray to them for help anymore.
At that time I will make a covenant
  for the good of my people.
I will make Israel my own.
  She will belong to me forever.
I will do to her what is right and fair.
  I will love her tenderly.
I will be faithful to her.
  And she will recognize me as the LORD.

"So at that time I will answer her,"
  announces the LORD.
"I will command the skies
  to send rain on the earth.
Then the earth will produce grain, olive oil and fresh wine.
  And Israel will be called Jezreel.
  That's because I will answer her prayers.
I will plant her in the land for myself.
  I will show my love to the one I called Not My Loved
    One.
I will say, 'You are my people'
  to those who were called Not My People.
  And they will say, 'You are my God.' "

People of Israel, listen to the LORD's message.
  He is bringing charges
  against you who live in Israel.

He says, "There is no faithfulness
  or love in the land.
  No one recognizes me as God.
People curse one another.
  They tell lies and commit murder.
  They steal.
They break all my laws.
  They keep spilling the blood of other people.
That is why the land is drying up.
  All those who live in it
  are getting weaker and weaker.
The wild animals and the birds in the sky are dying.
  So are the fish in the ocean.

"Israel, you are not faithful to me.
  But I do not want Judah to become guilty too.

"Israel's pride proves that they are guilty.
  The people of Ephraim trip and fall because they have
    sinned.
  Judah falls down along with them.
Israel will come to worship the LORD.
  They will bring their animals to offer as sacrifices.
But they will not find him.
  He has turned away from them.
They are not faithful to the LORD.
  Their children are not his.

"Ephraim will soon be crushed.
  The Assyrians will stomp all over them.
It will happen because they have made up their minds
  to chase after other gods.
I will be like a moth to Ephraim.
  I will cause Judah to rot away.

"The people of Ephraim saw how sick they were.
  The people of Judah saw that they were wounded.
Then Ephraim turned to Assyria for help.
  They sent gifts to the great King Tiglath-Pileser.

But he is not able to make you well.
　He can't heal your wounds.
I will be like a lion to Ephraim.
　I will attack Judah like a powerful lion.
I will tear them to pieces.
　I will drag them off.
Then I will leave them.
　No one will be able to save them.
I will go back to my lion's den.
　I will stay there until they pay the price for their sin.
Then they will turn to me.
　They will suffer so much
　that they will really want me to help them."

The people say, "Come.
　Let us return to the LORD.
He has torn us to pieces.
　But he will heal us.
He has wounded us.
　But he'll bandage our wounds.
After two days he will give us new life.
　On the third day he'll make us like new again.
　Then we will enjoy his blessing.
Let's recognize him as the LORD.
　Let's keep trying to know him.
You can be sure the sun will rise.
　And you can be just as sure the LORD will appear.
He will come to renew us like the winter rains.
　He will be like the spring rains that water the earth."

The LORD says,

"People of Judah, I have also appointed a time
　for you to be destroyed.

"My people have broken the covenant I made with them.
　They have refused to obey my law.
Israel shouts to me,
　'We recognize you as our God!'

But they have turned away from what is good.
  So an enemy will chase them.
My people appoint kings I do not want.
  They choose princes without my permission.
They use their silver and gold
    to make statues of gods.
    That is how they destroy themselves."

The time when God will punish you is coming.
  The day when he will judge you is near.
  I want Israel to know this.
You have committed many sins.
  And you hate me very much.
That's why you think the prophet is foolish.
  You think the person the LORD speaks through is
      crazy.
People of Ephraim, the prophet, along with my God,
  is warning you of danger.
But you set traps for him everywhere he goes.
  You hate him so much
  you even wait for him in God's house.
You have sunk very deep into sin,
  just as your people did at Gibeah long ago.
God will remember the evil things they have
      done.
  He will punish them for their sins.

Israel was like a spreading vine.
  They produced fruit for themselves.
As they grew more fruit,
  they built more altars.
As their land became richer,
  they made more beautiful the sacred stones they
      worshiped.
Their hearts are dishonest.
  So now they must pay for their sins.
The LORD will tear down their altars.
  He'll destroy their sacred stones.

The LORD says,

"Ephraim was like a well-trained young cow.
  It loved to thresh grain.
So I will put a yoke
  on its pretty neck.
I will make Ephraim do hard work.
  Judah also must plow.
So all the people of Jacob
  must break up the ground.
Your hearts are as hard as a field
  that has not been plowed.
If you change your ways,
  you will produce good crops.
So plant the seeds of doing what is right.
  Then you will harvest the fruit of your faithful love.
It is time to seek the LORD.
  When you do, he will come
  and shower his blessings on you.
But you have planted the seeds of doing what is wrong.
  So you have harvested the fruit of your evil conduct.
  You have had to eat the fruit of your lies.
You have trusted in your own strength.
  You have depended on your many soldiers.
But the roar of battle will come against you.
  All your forts will be completely destroyed.

"You are like a trader who uses dishonest scales.
  You love to cheat others.
People of Ephraim, you brag,
  "We are very rich.
  We've become wealthy.
And no one can prove we sinned
  to gain all this wealth."

The LORD says,

"People of Israel, I have been the LORD your God
  ever since you came out of Egypt.

You must not worship any god but me.
  You must not have any savior except me.
I took care of you in the desert.
  It was a land of burning heat.
I fed them until they were satisfied.
  Then they became proud.
  They forgot all about me.

"I will set these people free from the power of the grave.
  I will save them from death.
Death, where are your plagues?
  Grave, where is your power to destroy?"

Israel, return to the LORD your God.
  Your sins have destroyed you!
Tell the LORD you are turning away from your sins.
  Return to him.
Say to him,
  "Forgive us for all our sins.
Please be kind to us.
  Welcome us back to you.
  Then our lips will offer you our praise.
Assyria can't save us.
  We won't trust in our war horses.
Our own hands have made statues of gods.
  But we will never call them our gods again.
We are like children whose fathers have died.
  But you show us your tender love."

Then the LORD will answer,

"My people always wander away from me.
  But I will put an end to that.
My anger has turned away from them.
  Now I will love them freely.
I will be like the dew to Israel.
  They will bloom like a lily.
They will send their roots down deep
  like a cedar tree in Lebanon.

Once again my people will live
  in the safety of my shade.
  They will grow like grain.
They will bloom like vines.
  And Israel will be as famous
  as wine from Lebanon.
Ephraim will have nothing more to do with other gods.
  I will answer the prayers of my people.
  I will take good care of them."

If someone is wise, they will realize
  that what I've said is true.
If they have understanding,
  they will know what it means.
The ways of the LORD are right.
  People who are right with God live the way he wants
      them to.
  But those who refuse to obey him trip and fall.

remember what you read

1. What is something you noticed for the first time?

_____

_____

_____

_____

2. What questions did you have?

_____

_____

_____

_____

3. Was there anything that bothered you?

_____

_____

_____

_____

4. What did you learn about loving God?

_____

_____

_____

_____

5. What did you learn about loving others?

_____

_____

_____

_____

MICAH

introduction to Micah

God told the prophet Micah to warn the people of Jerusalem, the capital city of Judah, the southern kingdom of God's people. He warned that they would be destroyed for how they lived and how they had not kept the covenant agreement with God. He also warned that Samaria, the capital city of the northern kingdom of Israel, would be destroyed. But each time Micah spoke about things being destroyed, he also spoke about how God would bring back the people. Micah says to God, "You forgive your people when they do what is wrong. You don't stay angry forever. Instead you take delight in showing your faithful love to them."

A message from the LORD came to Micah. The message came while Jotham, Ahaz and Hezekiah were kings of Judah. This is the vision Micah saw concerning Samaria and Jerusalem. Here is what he said.

Listen to me, all you nations!
    Earth and everyone who lives in it, pay attention!
The LORD and King will be a witness against you.
    The Lord will speak from his holy temple in heaven.

The LORD is about to come down
    from his home in heaven.
    He rules over even the highest places on earth.
The mountains will melt under him
    like wax near a fire.

The valleys will be broken apart
  by water rushing down a slope.
All this will happen because
  Jacob's people have done what is wrong.
The people of Israel
  have committed many sins.
Who is to blame
  for the wrong things Jacob has done?
  Samaria!
Who is to blame for the high places
  where Judah's people worship other gods?
  Jerusalem!

So the LORD says,

"I will turn Samaria into a pile of trash.
  It will become a place for planting vineyards.
I will dump its stones down into the valley.
  And I will destroy it
  down to its very foundations.
All the statues of Samaria's gods
  will be broken to pieces.

I will weep and mourn because Samaria will be
    destroyed.
  I'll walk around barefoot and naked.
I'll bark like a wild dog.
  I'll hoot like an owl.
Samaria's plague can't be healed.
  The plague has spread to Judah.
It has spread right up to the gate of my people.
  It has spread to Jerusalem itself.
The wrong things Israel did
  were also done by you.

How terrible it will be for those
  who plan to harm others!

How terrible for those who make evil plans
   before they even get out of bed!
As soon as daylight comes,
   they carry out their plans.
   That's because they have the power to do it.
If they want fields or houses,
   they take them.
They cheat people out of their homes.
   They rob them of their property.

So the Lord says to them,

"I am planning to send trouble on you.
   You will not be able to save yourselves from it.
You will not live so proudly anymore.
   It will be a time of trouble.
At that time people will make fun of you.
   They will tease you by singing a song of sadness.
   They will pretend to be you and say,
'We are totally destroyed.
   Our enemies have divided up our land.
The Lord has taken it away from us!
   He has given our fields to those
   who turned against us.'"

"Don't prophesy," the people's prophets say.
   "Don't prophesy about bad things.
   Nothing shameful is going to happen to us."
People of Jacob, should anyone say,
   "The Lord is patient,
   so he wouldn't do things like that"?

The Lord replies, "What I promise brings good
     things
   to those who lead honest lives.
But lately my people have attacked one another
   as if they were enemies.

In the last days

the mountain where the Lord's temple is located will be
  famous.
  It will be the highest mountain of all.
It will be lifted up above the hills.
  And nations will go to it.

People from many nations will go there. They will say,

"Come, let us go up to the Lord's mountain.
  Let's go to the temple of Jacob's God.
He will teach us how we should live.
  Then we will live the way he wants us to."
The law of the Lord will be taught at Zion.
  His message will go out from Jerusalem.
He will judge between people from many nations.
  He'll settle problems among strong nations everywhere.
They will hammer their swords into plows.
  They'll hammer their spears into pruning tools.
Nations will not go to war against one another.
  They won't even train to fight anymore.
Everyone will have
  their own vine and fig tree.
And no one will make them afraid.
  That's what the Lord who rules over all has promised.
Other nations worship and trust in their gods.
  But we will worship and obey the Lord.
  He will be our God for ever and ever.

$\sim\!\!\infty\!\!\sim$

"The time is coming
  when I will gather those who are disabled,"
  announces the Lord.
"I will bring together those
  who were taken away as prisoners.
  I will gather those I have allowed to suffer.

I will make the disabled my faithful people.
　　I will make into a strong nation those driven away from
　　　　their homes.
I will rule over them on Mount Zion.
　　I will be their King from that time on and forever.
Jerusalem, you used to be
　　like a guard tower for my flock.
City of Zion, you used to be
　　a place of safety for my people.
The glorious kingdom you had before
　　will be given back to you.
　　Once again a king will rule over your people."

Jerusalem, you are being attacked.
　　So bring your troops together.
Our enemies have surrounded us.
　　They want to slap the face of Israel's ruler.

The Lord says,

"Bethlehem Ephrathah, you might not be
　　an important town in the nation of Judah.
But out of you will come for me
　　a ruler over Israel.
His family line goes back
　　to the early years of your nation.
It goes all the way back
　　to days of long ago."

The Lord will hand over his people to their enemies.
　　That will last until the pregnant woman bears her promised
　　　　son.
Then the rest of his relatives in Judah
　　will return to their land.

That promised son will stand firm
　　and be a shepherd for his flock.

The LORD will give him the strength to do it.
  The LORD his God will give him
  the authority to rule.
His people will live safely.
  His greatness will reach
  from one end of the earth to the other.
The Assyrians will march across our borders
  and attack our land.
  But the promised ruler will save us from them.

LORD, your power will win the battle
  over your enemies.
  All of them will be destroyed.

✧✧✧

Israel, listen to the LORD's message. He says to me,

"Stand up in court.
  Let the mountains serve as witnesses.
  Let the hills hear what you have to say."

Hear the LORD's case, you mountains.
  Listen, you age-old foundations of the earth.
The LORD has a case against his people Israel.
  He is bringing charges against them.

The LORD says,

"My people, what have I done to you?
  Have I made things too hard for you? Answer me.
I brought your people up out of Egypt.
  I set them free from the land
  where they were slaves.
I sent Moses to lead them.
  Aaron and Miriam helped him.
Remember how Balak, the king of Moab,
  planned to put a curse on your people.
But Balaam, the son of Beor,
  gave them a blessing instead.

Remember their journey from Shittim to Gilgal.
I want you to know
that I always do what is right."

The people of Israel say,

"What should we bring with us
when we go to worship the LORD?
What should we offer the God of heaven
when we bow down to him?
Should we take burnt offerings to him?
Should we sacrifice calves
that are a year old?
Will the LORD be pleased with thousands of
rams?
Will he take delight in 10,000 rivers of olive
oil?
Should we offer our oldest sons
for the wrong things we've done?
Should we sacrifice our own children
to pay for our sins?"

The LORD has shown you what is good.
He has told you what he requires of you.
You must act with justice.
You must love to show mercy.
And you must be humble as you live in the sight of
your God.

❧

LORD, be like a shepherd to your people.
Take good care of them.
They are your flock.
They live by themselves
in the safety of a forest.
Rich grasslands are all around them.
Let them eat grass in Bashan and Gilead
just as they did long ago.

The LORD says to his people,

"I showed you my wonders
  when you came out of Egypt long ago.
  In the same way, I will show them to you again."

When the nations see those wonders,
  they will be put to shame.
  All their power will be taken away from them.
They will be so amazed
  that they won't be able to speak or hear.
They'll be forced to eat dust like a snake.
  They'll be like creatures
  that have to crawl on the ground.
They'll come out of their dens
  trembling with fear.
They'll show respect for the LORD our God.
  They will also have respect for his people.
LORD, who is a God like you?
  You forgive sin.
You forgive your people
  when they do what is wrong.
You don't stay angry forever.
  Instead, you take delight in showing
  your faithful love to them.
Once again you will show loving concern for us.
  You will completely wipe out
  the evil things we've done.
You will throw all our sins
  into the bottom of the sea.
You will be faithful to Jacob's people.
  You will show your love
  to Abraham's children.
You will do what you promised to do for our people.
  You made that promise long ago.

remember what you read

1. What is something you noticed for the first time?

_____

_____

_____

_____

2. What questions did you have?

_____

_____

_____

_____

3. Was there anything that bothered you?

_____

_____

_____

_____

4. What did you learn about loving God?

_____

_____

_____

_____

5. What did you learn about loving others?

_____

_____

_____

_____

introduction to Isaiah, part 1

The prophet Isaiah spoke to several kings in Jerusalem. Just like other prophets, he was a "covenant messenger," who reminded the people what the agreement with God said. Isaiah also spoke about a time when everything would be made new with God's people. God would rule his people and they would obey him perfectly.

༄༄༄

Here is the vision about Judah and Jerusalem that Isaiah saw. It came to him when Uzziah, Jotham, Ahaz and Hezekiah were ruling. They were kings of Judah.

Listen to me, you heavens! Pay attention to me, earth!
The Lord has said,
"I raised children. I brought them up.
But they have refused to obey me.
The ox knows its master.
The donkey knows where its owner feeds it.
But Israel does not know me.
My people do not understand me."

How terrible it will be for this sinful nation!
They are loaded down with guilt.
They are people who do nothing but evil.
They are children who are always sinning.
They have deserted the Lord.
They have turned against the Holy One of Israel.

They have turned their backs on him.

"Do you think I need any more of your sacrifices?"
    asks the LORD.
"I have more than enough of your burnt offerings.
    I have more than enough of rams
    and the fat of your fattest animals.
I do not find any pleasure
    in the blood of your bulls, lambs and goats.
Who asked you to bring all these animals
    when you come to worship me?
Who asked you and your animals
    to walk all over my courtyards?
Stop bringing offerings that do not mean anything to me!
    I hate your incense.
I can't stand your worthless gatherings.
    I can't stand the way you celebrate your New Moon
        feasts,
    Sabbath days and special services.
Your New Moon feasts and your other appointed feasts
    I hate with my whole being.
They have become a heavy load to me.
    I am tired of carrying it.
You might spread out your hands toward me when you pray.
    But I do not look at you.
You might even offer many prayers.
    But I am not listening to them.
Your hands are covered with the blood of the people you
        have murdered.
    So wash and make yourselves clean.
Get your evil actions out of my sight!
    Stop doing what is wrong!
    Learn to do what is right!
Treat people fairly.
    Help those who are treated badly.
Stand up in court for children whose fathers have died.
    And do the same thing for widows.

"Come. Let us settle this matter,"
    says the LORD.
"Even though your sins are bright red,
    they will be as white as snow.
Even though they are deep red,
    they will be white like wool.
But you have to be willing to change and obey me.
    If you are, you will eat the good things that grow on the
        land.
But if you are not willing to obey me,
    you will be killed by swords."
The LORD has spoken.

Zion will be saved when justice is done.
    Those who are sorry for their sins will be saved
    when what is right is done.
But sinners and those who refuse to obey the LORD will
        be destroyed.
    And those who desert the LORD will die.

෴

Here is a vision that Isaiah, the son of Amoz, saw about Judah
and Jerusalem.

In the last days

the mountain where the LORD's temple is located will be
        famous.
    It will be the highest mountain of all.
It will be raised above the hills.
    All the nations will go to it.

People from many nations will go there. They will say,

"Come. Let us go up to the LORD's mountain.
    Let's go to the temple of Jacob's God.
He will teach us how we should live.
    Then we will live the way he wants us to."

The law of the LORD will be taught at Zion.
His message will go out from Jerusalem.
He will judge between the nations.
He'll settle problems among many of them.
They will hammer their swords into plows.
They'll hammer their spears into pruning tools.
Nations will not go to war against one another.
They won't even train to fight anymore.

People of Jacob, come.
Let us live the way the LORD has taught us to.

LORD, you have deserted the people of Jacob.
They are your people.
The land is full of false beliefs from the east.
The people practice evil magic, just as the Philistines do.
They do what ungodly people do.
Their land is full of silver and gold.
There is no end to their treasures.
Their land is full of horses.
There is no end to their chariots.
Their land is full of statues of gods.
Their people bow down to what their own hands have
made.
They bow down to what their fingers have shaped.
So people will be brought low.
Everyone will be made humble.
Do not forgive them.

Go and hide in caves in the rocks, you people!
Hide in holes in the ground.
Hide from the terrifying presence of the LORD!
Hide when he comes in glory and majesty!
Anyone who brags will be brought low.
Anyone who is proud will be made humble.
The LORD alone will be honored at that time.

Jerusalem is about to fall.
  And so is Judah.
They say and do things against the LORD.
  They dare to disobey him to his very face.
The look on their faces is a witness against them.
  They show off their sin, just as the people of Sodom did.
  They don't even try to hide it.
How terrible it will be for them!
  They have brought trouble on themselves.

Tell those who do what is right that things will go well with
    them.
  They will enjoy the results of the good things they've done.
But how terrible it will be for those who do what is evil!
  Trouble is about to fall on them.
  They will be paid back for the evil things they've done.

The LORD takes his place in court.
  He stands up to judge the people.
He judges the elders and leaders of his people.
  He says to them,
"My people are like a vineyard.
  You have destroyed them.
  The things you have taken from poor people are in your
    houses.
What do you mean by crushing my people?
  Why are you grinding the faces of the poor into the dirt?"
  announces the Lord. He is the LORD who rules over all.

❧

At that time Israel's king will be beautiful and glorious. He will
be called The Branch of the LORD. The fruit of the land will be the
pride and glory of those who are still left alive in Israel. Those who
are left in Zion will be called holy. They will be recorded among
those who are alive in Jerusalem. The Lord will wash away the sin
of the women in Zion. He will clean up the blood that was spilled
there. He will judge those who spilled that blood. His burning

anger will blaze out at them. Then the LORD will create over Jerusalem a cloud of smoke by day. He will also create a glow of flaming fire at night. The cloud and fire will appear over all of Mount Zion. They will also appear over the people who gather together there. The LORD's glory will be like a tent over everything. It will cover the people and give them shade from the hot sun all day long. It will be a safe place where they can hide from storms and rain.

I will sing a song for the LORD.
   He is the one I love.
   It's a song about his vineyard Israel.
The one I love had a vineyard.
   It was on a hillside that had rich soil.
He dug up the soil and removed its stones.
   He planted the very best vines in it.
He built a lookout tower there.
   He also cut out a winepress for it.
Then he kept looking for a crop of good grapes.
   But the vineyard produced only bad fruit.

So the LORD said, "People of Jerusalem and Judah,
   you be the judge between me and my vineyard.
What more could I have done for my vineyard?
   I did everything I could.
I kept looking for a crop of good grapes.
   So why did it produce only bad ones?
Now I will tell you
   what I am going to do to my vineyard.
I will take away its fence.
   And the vineyard will be destroyed.
I will break down its wall.
   And people will walk all over my vineyard.
I will turn my vineyard into a dry and empty desert.
   It will not be pruned or taken care of.
   Thorns and bushes will grow there.
I will command the clouds
   not to rain on it."

The vineyard of the Lᴏʀᴅ who rules over all
  is the nation of Israel.
The people of Judah
  are the vines he took delight in.
He kept looking for them to do what is fair.
  But all he saw was blood being spilled.
He kept looking for them to do what is right.
  But all he heard were cries of suffering.

ᗛᗛᗛ

I heard the Lᴏʀᴅ who rules over all announce a message. He said,

How terrible it will be for those who continue to sin
  and lie about it!
How terrible for those who keep on doing what is evil
  as if they were tied to it!
How terrible for those who say,
  "Let God hurry up and do what he says he will.
  We want to see it happen.
Let us see the plan of the Holy One of Israel.
  We want to know what it is."

How terrible it will be for those who say
  that what is evil is good!
How terrible for those who say
  that what is good is evil!
How terrible for those who say
  that darkness is light
  and light is darkness!
How terrible for those who say
  that what is bitter is sweet
  and what is sweet is bitter!

How terrible it will be for those who think they are wise!
  How terrible for those who think they are really clever!

How terrible for those
  who take money to set guilty people free!

How terrible for those
  who don't treat good people fairly!
Flames of fire burn up straw.
  Dry grass sinks down into those flames.
Evil people will be like plants whose roots rot away.
  They will be like flowers that are blown away like dust.
That's because they have said no to the law of the LORD who
    rules over all.
  They have turned against the message of the Holy One of
    Israel.
So the LORD is angry with his people.
  He raises his hand against them and strikes them down.

remember what you read

1. What is something you noticed for the first time?

_____

_____

_____

_____

2. What questions did you have?

_____

_____

_____

_____

3. Was there anything that bothered you?

_____

_____

_____

_____

4. What did you learn about loving God?

_____

_____

_____

_____

5. What did you learn about loving others?

_____

_____

_____

_____

introduction to Isaiah, part 2

Today's reading begins with God calling Isaiah to speak for him. God provided signs and words of hope for the people. This was even though he destroyed parts of Judah because they trusted in other nations to take care of them instead of trusting God to do so.

In the year that King Uzziah died, I saw the Lord. He was seated on his throne. His long robe filled the temple. He was highly honored. Above him were seraphs. Each of them had six wings. With two wings they covered their faces. With two wings they covered their feet. And with two wings they were flying. They were calling out to one another. They were saying,

"Holy, holy, holy is the Lord who rules over all.
    The whole earth is full of his glory."

The sound of their voices caused the stone doorframe to shake. The temple was filled with smoke.

"How terrible it is for me!" I cried out. "I'm about to be destroyed! My mouth speaks sinful words. And I live among people who speak sinful words. Now I have seen the King with my own eyes. He is the Lord who rules over all."

A seraph flew over to me. He was holding a hot coal. He had used tongs to take it from the altar. He touched my mouth with the coal. He said, "This has touched your lips. Your guilt has been taken away. Your sin has been paid for."

Then I heard the voice of the Lord. He said, "Who will I send? Who will go for us?"

I said, "Here I am. Send me!"

So he said, "Go and speak to these people. Tell them,

" 'You will hear but never understand.
    You will see but never know what you are seeing.'
Make the hearts of these people stubborn.
    Plug up their ears.
    Close their eyes.
Otherwise they might see with their eyes.
    They might hear with their ears.
    They might understand with their hearts.
And they might turn to me and be healed."

༄༄༄

Ahaz was king of Judah. Rezin was king of Aram. And Pekah was king of Israel. Rezin and Pekah marched up to fight against Jerusalem. But they couldn't overpower it. Ahaz was the son of Jotham and the grandson of Uzziah. Pekah was the son of Remaliah.

The royal family of Ahaz was told, "The army of Aram has joined forces with Ephraim's army." So the hearts of Ahaz and his people trembled with fear. They shook just as trees in the forest shake when the wind blows through them.

The LORD said to Isaiah, "Go out and see Ahaz. Take your son Shear-Jashub with you. Meet Ahaz at the end of the channel that brings water from the Upper Pool. It is on the road to the Washerman's Field. Tell Ahaz, 'Be careful. Stay calm. Do not be afraid. Do not lose hope because of the great anger of Rezin, Aram and the son of Remaliah. After all, they are nothing but two pieces of smoking firewood. Aram, Ephraim and Remaliah's son have planned to destroy you. They said, "Let's march into Judah and attack it. Let's tear everything down. Then we can share the land among ourselves. And we can make Tabeel's son king over it." But I am the LORD and King. I say,

" ' "That will not happen.
    It will not take place.

The capital of Aram is Damascus.
    And the ruler of Damascus is only Rezin.
Do not worry about the people of Ephraim.
    They will be too crushed to be considered a people.
    That will happen before 65 years are over.
The capital of Ephraim is Samaria.
    And the ruler of Samaria is only Remaliah's son.
If you do not stand firm in your faith,
    you will not stand at all." ' "

The Lord spoke to Ahaz through Isaiah again. He said, "I am the Lord your God. Ask me to give you a sign. It can be anything in the deepest grave or in the highest heaven."

But Ahaz said, "I won't ask. I won't test the Lord."

Then Isaiah said, "Listen, you members of the royal family of David! Isn't it enough for you to test the patience of human beings? Are you also going to test the patience of my God? The Lord himself will give you a sign. The virgin is going to have a baby. She will give birth to a son. And he will be called Immanuel. He will still be very young when he can decide between right and wrong. Even before then, the lands of the two kings you fear will be ruined. The Lord will also bring the king of Assyria against you. And he will bring him against your people and the whole royal family. That will be a time of trouble. It will be unlike any since the people of Ephraim broke away from Judah."

～～～

There are people who get messages from those who have died. But these people only whisper words that are barely heard. Suppose someone tells you to ask for advice from these people. Shouldn't you ask for advice from your God instead? People who don't speak in keeping with these words will have no hope in the morning. They'll see terrible sadness. They'll be driven into total darkness.

The people who are now living in darkness
    will see a great light.

They are now living in a very dark land.
  But a light will shine on them.
Lord, you will make our nation larger.
  You will increase their joy.
They will show you how glad they are.
  They will be as glad as people are at harvest time.
A child will be born to us.
  A son will be given to us.
  He will rule over us.
And he will be called
  Wonderful Adviser and Mighty God.
He will also be called Father Who Lives Forever
  and Prince Who Brings Peace.
There will be no limit to how great his authority is.
  The peace he brings will never end.
He will rule on David's throne
  and over his kingdom.
  He will make the kingdom strong and secure.
His rule will be based on what is fair and right.
  It will last forever.
The Lord's great love will make sure that happens.
  He rules over all.

∽∬∾

The Lord says, "How terrible it will be for the people of
    Assyria!
  They are the war club that carries out my anger.
I will send them against the ungodly nation of Judah.
  I will order them to fight against my own people.
  My people make me angry.
I will order Assyria to take their goods and carry them away.
  I will order Assyria to walk on my people
  as if they were walking on mud.
But that is not what the king of Assyria plans.
  It is not what he has in mind.
His purpose is to destroy many nations.
  His purpose is to put an end to them.

The Lord will finish everything he has planned to do against
Mount Zion and Jerusalem. Then he'll say, "Now I will punish the
king of Assyria. I will punish him because his heart and his eyes
are so proud. The king of Assyria says,

" 'By my power
   I have taken over all these nations.
I am very wise.
   I have great understanding.
I have wiped out the borders between nations.
   I've taken their treasures.
   Like a great hero I've brought their kings under my control.
I've taken the wealth of the nations.
   It was as easy as reaching into a bird's nest.
I've gathered the riches of all these countries.
   It was as easy as gathering eggs
   that have been left in a nest.

⚬⚬⚬

In days to come, some people will still be left alive in Israel.
   They will be from Jacob's family line.
But they won't depend any longer on
   the nation that struck them down.
Instead, they will truly depend on the Lord.
   He is the Holy One of Israel.
The people of Jacob who are still alive
   will return to the Mighty God.
Israel, your people might be as many as the grains of sand by
      the sea.
   But only a few of them will return.
The Lord has handed down a death sentence.
   He will destroy his people.
   What he does is right.
The Lord who rules over all will carry out his sentence.
   The Lord will destroy the whole land.

⚬⚬⚬

Jesse's family is like a tree that has been cut down.
    A new little tree will grow from its stump.
    From its roots a Branch will grow and produce fruit.
The Spirit of the Lord will rest on that Branch.
    The Spirit will help him to be wise and understanding.
The Spirit will help him make wise plans and carry them out.
    The Spirit will help him know the Lord and have respect for
        him.
The Branch will take delight
    in respecting the Lord.

He will not judge things only by the way they look.
    He won't make decisions based simply on what people say.
He will always do what is right
    when he judges those who are in need.
He'll be completely fair
    when he makes decisions about poor people.
When he commands that people be punished,
    it will happen.
When he orders that evil people be put to death,
    it will take place.
He will put on godliness as if it were his belt.
    He'll wear faithfulness around his waist.

Wolves will live with lambs.
    Leopards will lie down with goats.
Calves and lions will eat together.
    And little children will lead them around.
Cows will eat with bears.
    Their little ones will lie down together.
    And lions will eat straw like oxen.
A baby will play near a hole where cobras live.
    A young child will put its hand into a nest
    where poisonous snakes live.
None of those animals will harm or destroy anything or anyone
    on my holy mountain of Zion.
The oceans are full of water.
    In the same way, the earth will be filled
    with the knowledge of the Lord

At that time, here is what the man who is called the Root of Jesse will do. He will be like a banner that brings nations together. They will come to him. And the place where he rules will be glorious. At that time the Lord will reach out his hand. He will gather his people a second time. He will bring back those who are left alive. He'll bring them back from Assyria, Lower Egypt, Upper Egypt and Cush. He'll bring them from Elam, Babylon and Hamath. He will also bring them from the islands of the Mediterranean Sea.

᷇᷇᷇

In days to come, the people of Israel will sing,

"Lord, we will praise you.
    You were angry with us.
But now your anger has turned away from us.
    And you have brought us comfort.
God, you are the one who saves us.
    We will trust in you.
    Then we won't be afraid.
Lord, you are the one who gives us strength.
    You are the one who keeps us safe.
    Lord, you have saved us."
People of Israel, he will save you.
    That will bring you joy like water brought up from wells.

In days to come, the people of Israel will sing,

"Give praise to the Lord. Make his name known.
    Tell the nations what he has done.
    Announce how honored he is.
Sing to the Lord. He has done glorious things.
    Let it be known all over the world.
People of Zion, give a loud shout!
    Sing for joy!
The Holy One of Israel is among you.
    And he is great."

remember what you read

1. What is something you noticed for the first time?

_____

_____

_____

_____

2. What questions did you have?

_____

_____

_____

_____

3. Was there anything that bothered you?

_____

_____

_____

_____

4. What did you learn about loving God?

_____

_____

_____

_____

5. What did you learn about loving others?

_____

_____

_____

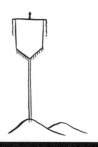

ISAIAH, PART 3

introduction to Isaiah, part 3

God always meant for all people to love him and serve him. The nations around Israel and Judah did not have a promise from God the way they did. But God still expected the nations to treat each other well and respect others. Isaiah spoke for God against a number of nations because of the ways they chose to live.

Here is the prophecy against Babylon that Isaiah, the son of Amoz, saw.

Lift up a banner on the top of a bare hill.
Shout to the enemy soldiers.
Wave for them to enter the gates
that are used by the nobles of Babylon.
The LORD has commanded the soldiers he prepared for battle.
He has sent for them to carry out his anger against
Babylon.
They will be happy when he wins the battle for them.

The day of the LORD is coming.
It will be a terrible day.
The LORD's burning anger will blaze out.
He will make the land dry and empty.
He'll destroy the sinners in it.
The LORD will punish the world because it is so evil.
He will punish evil people for their sins.

He'll put an end to the bragging of those who are proud.
　　He'll bring down the pride of those who don't show any
　　　　pity.
The Lord who rules over all will show how angry he is.
　　At that time his burning anger will blaze out.

The Lord will stir up the Medes to attack the Babylonians.
　　They aren't interested in getting silver.
　　They don't want gold.
Instead, they will use their bows and arrows
　　to strike down the young men.
They won't even show any mercy to babies.
　　They won't take pity on children.
The city of Babylon is the jewel of kingdoms.
　　It is the pride and glory of the Babylonians.
But God will destroy it
　　just as he did Sodom and Gomorrah.
No one will ever live in Babylon again.
　　No one will live there for all time to come.
Those who wander in the desert will never set up their
　　　　tents there.
　　Shepherds will never rest their flocks there.

The Lord will show tender love toward Jacob's people.
　　Once again he will choose Israel.
　　He'll give them homes in their own land.
Outsiders will join them.
　　They and the people of Jacob will become one
　　　　people.
Nations will help Israel
　　return to their own land.

The Lord will put an end to Israel's suffering and trouble. They
will no longer be forced to do hard labor. At that time, they will
make fun of the king of Babylon. They will say,

"See how the one who crushed others has fallen!
　　See how his anger has come to an end!

The Lord has taken away the authority of evil people.
  He has broken the power of rulers.
When they became angry, they struck down nations.
  Their blows never stopped.
In their anger they brought nations under their control.
  They attacked them again and again.
All the lands now enjoy peace and rest.
  They break out into singing.
Even the juniper trees show how happy they are.
  The cedar trees of Lebanon celebrate too.
They say, 'Babylon, you have fallen.
  Now no one comes and cuts us down.'

"King of Babylon, you thought you were the bright morning
    star.
  But now you have fallen from heaven!
You once brought down nations.
  But now you have been thrown down to the earth!
You said in your heart,
  'I will go up to the heavens.
I'll raise my throne
  above the stars of God.
I'll sit as king on the mountain where the gods meet.
  I'll set up my throne on the highest slopes of Mount
    Zaphon.
I will rise above the tops of the clouds.
  I'll make myself like the Most High God.'
But now you have been brought down to the place of the
    dead.
  You have been thrown into the deepest part of the pit.

That's how the Lord carries out his plan all over the world.
  That's how he reaches out his powerful hand to punish all
    the nations.
The Lord who rules over all has planned it.
  Who can stop him?
He has reached out his powerful hand.
  Who can keep him from using it?

Here is a prophecy against Moab that the LORD gave me.

The people of Dibon go up to their temple to worship.
    They go to their high places to weep.
    The people of Moab cry over the cities of Nebo and
        Medeba.
All their heads are shaved.
    All their beards have been cut off.
In the streets they wear the rough clothing people wear when
        they're sad.
    On their roofs and in the market places
    all of them are crying.
They fall down flat with their faces toward the ground.
    And they weep.
The people of Heshbon and Elealeh cry out.
    Their voices are heard all the way to Jahaz.
So the fighting men of Moab cry out.
    Their hearts are weak.

People of Moab, send lambs as a gift
    to the ruler of Judah.
The Moabites say to the rulers of Judah,
    "Make up your mind. Make a decision.
Cover us with your shadow.
    Make it like night even at noon.
Hide those of us who are running away.
    Don't turn them over to their enemies.
Let those who have run away from Moab stay with you.
    Keep them safe from those who are trying to destroy them."

Those who crush others will be destroyed.
    The killing will stop.
    The attackers will disappear from the earth.
A man from the royal house of David will sit on Judah's
        throne.
    He will rule with faithful love.

When he judges he will do what is fair.
    He will be quick to do what is right.

We have heard all about Moab's pride.
    We have heard how very proud they are.
    They think they are so much better than others.
They brag about themselves.
    But all their bragging is nothing but empty words.

My heart mourns over Moab like a song of sadness played
        on a harp.
    Deep down inside me I mourn over Kir Hareseth.
Moab's people go to their high place to pray.
    But all they do is wear themselves out.
    Their god Chemosh can't help them at all.

⚮

In days to come, people will look to their Maker for help.
    They will turn their eyes to the Holy One of Israel.
They won't trust in the altars
    they made with their own hands.
They won't pay any attention to the poles they used
    to worship the female god named Asherah.
And they won't depend on the incense altars
    they made with their own fingers.

At that time the strong cities in Israel will be deserted. They will be as they were when the Israelites drove the Canaanites away. They will be like places that are taken over by bushes and weeds. The whole land will become dry and empty.

Israel, you have forgotten God, who saves you.
    You have not remembered the Rock, who keeps you safe.

How terrible it will be for the nations that attack us!
    The noise of their armies is like the sound of the ocean.
How terrible it will be for the nations who fight against us!
    They are as loud as huge waves crashing on the shore.

They sound like the roar of rushing waters.
But when the LORD speaks out against them, they run far away.
In the evening, the nations terrify us.
But before morning comes, they are gone.
That's what happens to those who steal our goods.
That's what happens to those who take what belongs to us.

∽✢∾

Here is a prophecy against Egypt that the LORD gave me.

The LORD is coming to Egypt.
He's riding on a cloud that moves very fast.
The statues of the gods in Egypt tremble with fear because of him.
The hearts of the people there melt with fear.

The LORD says, "I will stir up one Egyptian against another.
Relatives will fight against relatives.
Neighbors will fight against one another.
Cities will fight against cities.
Kingdoms will fight against one another.
The people of Egypt will lose hope.
I will keep them from doing what they plan to do.
They will ask their gods for advice.
They will turn to the spirits of dead people for help.
They will go to people who get messages from those who have died.
They will ask for advice from people who talk to the spirits of the dead.
I will hand the Egyptians over
to a mean and unkind master.
A powerful king will rule over them," announces the LORD.
He is the LORD who rules over all.

Pharaoh, where are your wise men now?
Let them tell you
what the LORD who rules over all
has planned against Egypt.

At that time the people of five cities in Egypt will worship the Lord. He is the Lord who rules over all. They will use the Hebrew language when they worship him. They will promise to be faithful to him. One of those cities will be called the City of the Sun.

At that time there will be a wide road from Egypt to Assyria. The people of Assyria will go to Egypt. And the people of Egypt will go to Assyria. The people of Egypt and Assyria will worship the Lord together. At that time Egypt, Assyria and Israel will be a blessing to the whole earth. The Lord who rules over all will bless those three nations. He will say, "Let the Egyptians be blessed. They are my people. Let the Assyrians be blessed. My hands created them. And let the Israelites be blessed. They are my very own people."

ᘒᘔᖇ

Here is a prophecy against Jerusalem that the Lord gave me. Jerusalem is also known as the Valley of Vision.

People of Jerusalem, what's the matter with you?
   Why have all of you gone up on the roofs of your houses?
Why is your town so full of noise?
   Why is your city so full of the sound of wild parties?

At that time, you depended
   on the weapons in the Palace of the Forest of Lebanon.
You saw that the walls of the City of David
   were broken through in many places.
You stored up water
   in the Lower Pool.
You picked out the weaker buildings in Jerusalem.
   You tore them down and used their stones
   to strengthen the city walls against attack.
You built a pool between the two walls.
   You used it to save the water
   that was running down from the Old Pool.
But you didn't look to the God who made it all possible.
   You didn't pay any attention to the God
   who planned everything long ago.

The LORD who rules over all
  called out to you at that time.
The Lord told you to weep and cry.
  He told you to tear your hair out.
  And he told you to put on the rough clothing people wear
    when they're sad.
Instead, you are enjoying yourselves at wild parties!
  You are killing cattle and sheep.
  You are eating their meat and drinking wine.
You are saying, "Let's eat and drink,
  because tomorrow we'll die."

I heard the LORD who rules over all speaking. "Your sin can never be paid for as long as you live," says the Lord.

remember what you read

1. What is something you noticed for the first time?

_____

_____

_____

_____

2. What questions did you have?

_____

_____

_____

_____

3. Was there anything that bothered you?

_____

_____

_____

_____

4. What did you learn about loving God?

_____

_____

_____

_____

5. What did you learn about loving others?

_____

_____

_____

_____

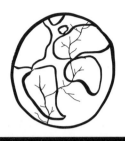

introduction to Isaiah, part 4

Isaiah has been talking about kingdoms and nations. Now he's going to talk about all of God's creation. Everything, from people to all of nature, will be judged. Isaiah has talked about very big events, like new governments or having to leave their homelands. He wants people to understand how serious he is. So he talks about things that seem solid and permanent, like the earth and the stars, getting damaged. This helped explain events the people couldn't believe were happening. In our language, we might call these "earth-shattering" events, even though the ground itself doesn't really shatter, or break open. After talking about God's judging his creation, Isaiah says Israel will return to their land as a united nation and all people will live with joy.

In the second part of today's reading, Isaiah says God will judge Judah for trusting other nations to protect them instead of trusting God.

The Lord is going to completely destroy everything on earth.
    He will twist its surface.
    He'll scatter those who live on it.
Priests and people alike will suffer.
    So will masters and their servants.
    And so will women and their female servants.
Sellers and buyers alike will suffer.
    So will those who borrow and those who lend.
    And so will those who owe money and those who lend it.

The earth will be completely destroyed.
    Everything of value will be taken out of it.
That's what the LORD has said.

The earth will dry up completely.
    The world will dry up and waste away.
    The heavens will fade away along with the earth.
The earth is polluted by its people.
    They haven't obeyed the laws of the LORD.
They haven't done what he told them to do.
    They've broken the covenant that will last
        forever.
So the LORD will send a curse on the earth.
    Its people will pay for what they've done.
They will be burned up.
    Very few of them will be left.

Those who are left alive will shout for joy.
    People from the west will praise the LORD because
        he is the King.
So give glory to him, you who live in the east.
    Honor the name of the LORD, you who are in the
        islands of the sea.
    He is the God of Israel.
From one end of the earth to the other we hear singing.
    People are saying,
    "Give glory to the God who always does what is
        right."

But I said, "I feel very bad.
    I'm getting weaker and weaker.
    How terrible it is for me!
People turn against one another.
    They can't be trusted.
    So they turn against one another."

The LORD will open the windows of the skies.
    He will flood the land.
    The foundations of the earth will shake.

The earth will be broken up.
  It will split open.
  It will be shaken to pieces.
The earth will be unsteady like someone who is drunk.
  It will sway like a tent in the wind.
Its sin will weigh so heavily on it that it will fall.
  It will never get up again.

At that time the LORD will punish
  the spiritual forces of evil in the heavens above.
  He will also punish the kings on the earth below.
They will be brought together
  like prisoners in chains.
They'll be locked up in prison.
  After many days the LORD will punish them.
The LORD who rules over all will rule
  on Mount Zion in Jerusalem.
The elders of the city will be there.
  They will see his great glory.
His rule will be so glorious that the sun and moon
  will be too ashamed to shine.

෴

LORD, you are my God.
  I will honor you.
  I will praise your name.
You have been perfectly faithful.
  You have done wonderful things.
  You had planned them long ago.
You have turned cities into piles of trash.
  You have pulled down the high walls that were around
    them.
You have destroyed our enemies' forts.
  They will never be rebuilt.
Powerful nations will honor you.
  Even sinful people from their cities will have respect for
    you.

Poor people have come to you for safety.
　You have kept needy people safe when they were in trouble.
You have been a place to hide when storms came.
　You have been a shade from the heat of the sun.

On Mount Zion the Lord who rules over all will prepare
　a feast for all the nations.
The best and richest foods
　and the finest aged wines will be served.
On that mountain the Lord will destroy
　the veil of sadness that covers all the nations.
He will destroy the gloom that is spread over everyone.
　He will swallow up death forever.
The Lord and King will wipe away the tears
　from everyone's face.
He will remove the shame of his people
　from the whole earth.
The Lord has spoken.

At that time they will say,

"He is our God.
　We trusted in him, and he saved us.
He is the Lord. We trusted in him.
　Let us be filled with joy because he saved us."

☙❀❧

The Lord's people are making fun of him. They say,
　"Who does he think he's trying to teach?
　Who does he think he's explaining his message to?
Is it to children who do not need their mother's milk
　　anymore?
　Is it to those who have just been taken from her breast?
Here is how he teaches.
　Do this and do that.
There is a rule for this and a rule for that.
　Learn a little here and learn a little there."

All right then, these people won't listen to me.
  So God will speak to them.
He will speak by using people who speak unfamiliar
    languages.
  He will speak by using the mouths of strangers.
He said to his people,
  "I am offering you a resting place.
  Let those who are tired rest."
He continued, "I am offering you a place of peace and
    quiet."
  But they wouldn't listen.
So then, here is what the LORD's message will become to
    them.
  Do this and do that.
There is a rule for this and a rule for that.
  Learn a little here and learn a little there.
So when they try to go forward,
  they'll fall back and be wounded.
  They'll be trapped and captured.

Listen to the LORD's message,
  you who make fun of the truth.
  Listen, you who rule over these people in Jerusalem.
You brag, "We have entered into a covenant with the
    place of the dead.
  We have made an agreement with the grave.
When a terrible plague comes to punish us,
  it can't touch us.
That's because we depend on lies to keep us safe.
  We hide behind what isn't true."

So the LORD and King speaks. He says,

"Look! I am laying a stone in Zion.
  It is a stone that has been tested.
It is the most important stone for a firm foundation.
  The one who depends on that stone will never be
    shaken.

I will use a measuring line to prove that you have not been
    fair.
  I will use a plumb line to prove that you have not done
    what is right.
Hail will sweep away the lies you depend on to keep you safe.
  Water will flood your hiding place.
Your covenant with death will be called off.
  The agreement you made with the place of the dead will
    not stand.
When the terrible plague comes to punish you,
  you will be struck down by it.
As often as it comes, it will carry you away.
  Morning after morning, day and night,
    it will come to punish you."

ᘯᘯᘯ

The Lord says,

"These people worship me only with their words.
  They honor me by what they say.
  But their hearts are far away from me.
Their worship doesn't mean anything to me.
  They teach nothing but human rules that they have been
    taught.
So once more I will shock these people
  with many wonderful acts.
I will destroy the wisdom of those who think they are so
    wise.
  I will do away with the cleverness of those who think they
    are so smart."
How terrible it will be for people who try hard
  to hide their plans from the LORD!
They do their work in darkness.
  They think, "Who sees us? Who will know?"
They turn everything upside down.
  How silly they are to think that potters are like the clay
    they work with!

Can what is made say to the one who made it,
　"You didn't make me"?
Can the pot say to the potter,
　"You don't know anything"?

Long ago the Lord saved Abraham from trouble. Now he says to Jacob's people,

"You will not be ashamed anymore.
　Your faces will no longer grow pale with fear.
You will see your children living among you.
　I myself will give you those children.
Then you will honor my name.
　You will recognize how holy I am.
　I am the Holy One of Jacob.
You will have great respect for me.
　I am the God of Israel.
I will give understanding to you
　who find yourselves going astray.
You who are always speaking against others
　will accept what I teach you."

☙

"How terrible it will be for these stubborn children of mine!"
　announces the Lord.
"How terrible for those who carry out plans that did not
　　come from me!
　Their agreement with Egypt did not come from my Spirit.
　So they pile up one sin on top of another.
They go down to Egypt
　without asking me for advice.
They look to Pharaoh to help them.
　They ask Egypt to keep them safe.

The Lord said to me, "Go now.
　Write on a tablet for the people of Judah
　what I am about to say.

Also write it on a scroll.
  In days to come
  it will be a witness that lasts forever.
That's because these people of Judah refuse to
      obey me.
  They are children who tell lies.
  They will not listen to what I want to teach them.
They say to the seers,
  'Don't see any more visions!'
They say to the prophets,
  'Don't give us any more visions of what is right!
Tell us pleasant things.
  Prophesy things we want to hear even if they aren't
      true.
Get out of our way!
  Get off our path!
  Keep the Holy One of Israel away from us!' "

So the Holy One of Israel speaks. He says,

"You have turned your backs on what I have said.
  You have depended on telling people lies.
  You have crushed others.
Those sins are like cracks in a high wall.
  They get bigger and bigger.
Suddenly the wall breaks apart.
  Then it quickly falls down.

The Lord and King is the Holy One of Israel. He says,

"You will find peace and rest
  when you turn away from your sins and depend on me.
You will receive the strength you need
  when you stay calm and trust in me.
  But you do not want to do what I tell you to.
You said, 'No. We'll escape on horses.'
  So you will have to escape!
You said, 'We'll ride off on fast horses.'
  So those who chase you will use faster horses!

But the LORD wants to have mercy on you.
  So he will rise up to give you his tender love.
The LORD is a God who is always fair.
  Blessed are all those who wait for him to act!

⁓⁓⁓

A king will come who will do what is right.
  His officials will govern fairly.
Each official will be like a place to get out of the wind.
  He will be like a place to hide from storms.
He'll be like streams of water flowing in the desert.
  He'll be like the shadow of a huge rock in a dry and thirsty
    land.

Then the eyes of those who see won't be closed anymore.
  The ears of those who hear will listen to the truth.
People who are afraid will know and understand.
  Tongues that stutter will speak clearly.
Foolish people won't be considered noble anymore.
  Those who are worthless won't be highly respected.
Foolish people say foolish things.
  Their minds are set on doing evil things.
They don't do what is right.
  They tell lies about the LORD.
They don't give hungry people any food.
  They don't let thirsty people have any water.
Those who are worthless use sinful methods.
  They make evil plans against poor people.
They destroy them with their lies.
  They do it even when those people are right.
But those who are noble make noble plans.
  And by doing noble things they succeed.

remember what you read

1. What is something you noticed for the first time?

_____

_____

_____

_____

2. What questions did you have?

_____

_____

_____

_____

3. Was there anything that bothered you?

_____

_____

_____

_____

4. What did you learn about loving God?

_____

_____

_____

_____

5. What did you learn about loving others?

_____

_____

_____

_____

introduction to Isaiah, part 5

Today's reading again shares how God sees his whole creation. He will judge all the people who do evil things. But he will also make his whole creation new.

Then Isaiah tells how King Hezekiah of Judah became so sick he was about to die. Even though Hezekiah was a good king who followed the covenant laws, Isaiah told how God would still send Judah away from their land as judgment for their evil living.

Nations, come near and listen to me!
   Pay attention to what I'm about to say.
Let the earth and everything in it listen.
   Let the world and everything that comes out of it pay
     attention.
The LORD is angry with all the nations.
   His anger is against all their armies.
He will totally destroy them.
   He will have them killed.
Those who are killed won't be buried.
   Their dead bodies will be thrown on the ground.
They will stink.
   Their blood will cover the mountains.
All the stars in the sky will vanish.
   The heavens will be rolled up like a scroll.

All the stars in the sky will fall like dried-up leaves from a
    vine.
    They will drop like wrinkled figs from a fig tree.

The desert and the dry ground will be glad.
    The dry places will be full of joy.
    Flowers will grow there.
Like the first crocus in the spring,
    the desert will bloom with flowers.
    It will be very glad and shout for joy.
Everyone will see the glory of the Lord.
    They will see the beauty of our God.

Strengthen the hands of those who are weak.
    Help those whose knees give way.
Say to those whose hearts are afraid,
    "Be strong and do not fear.
Your God will come.
    He will pay your enemies back.
    He will come to save you."

Then the eyes of those who are blind will be opened.
    The ears of those who can't hear will be unplugged.
Those who can't walk will leap like a deer.
    And those who can't speak will shout for joy.
Water will pour out in dry places.
    Streams will flow in the desert.
The burning sand will become a pool of water.
    The thirsty ground will become bubbling springs.
In the places where wild dogs once lay down,
    tall grass and papyrus will grow.

A wide road will go through the land.
    It will be called the Way of Holiness.
    Only those who lead a holy life can use it.
    "Unclean" and foolish people can't walk on it.

Only people who have been set free will walk on it.
   Those the LORD has saved will return to their land.
They will sing as they enter the city of Zion.
   Joy that lasts forever will be
   like beautiful crowns on their heads.
They will be filled with gladness and joy.
   Sorrow and sighing will be gone.

ᔿᔿᔿ

Sennacherib attacked and captured all the cities of Judah that had high walls around them. It was in the 14th year of the rule of Hezekiah. Sennacherib was king of Assyria. He sent his field commander from Lachish to King Hezekiah at Jerusalem. He sent him along with a large army.

   " 'Sennacherib is the great king of Assyria. He says, "Why are you putting your faith in what your king says? You say you have a military plan. You say you have a strong army. But your words don't mean anything. Who are you depending on? Why don't you want to stay under my control? Look, I know you are depending on Egypt. Why are you doing that? Egypt is nothing but a broken papyrus stem. Try leaning on it. It will only cut your hand. Pharaoh, the king of Egypt, is just like that to everyone who depends on him. But suppose you say to me, 'We are depending on the LORD our God.' Didn't Hezekiah remove your god's high places and altars? Didn't Hezekiah say to the people of Judah and Jerusalem, 'You must worship at the altar in Jerusalem'? The LORD himself told me to march out against your country. He told me to destroy it." ' "

When King Hezekiah heard what the field commander had said, he tore his clothes. He put on the rough clothing people wear when they're sad. Then he went into the LORD's temple.

King Hezekiah's officials came to Isaiah. Then he said to them, "Tell your master, 'The LORD says, "Do not be afraid of what you have heard. The officers who are under the king of Assyria have spoken evil things against me. Listen! I will send him news from

his own country. It will make him want to return home. There I
will have him cut down by a sword." ' "

During that time Sennacherib received a report. He was told that
Tirhakah was marching out to fight against him. Tirhakah was the
king of Cush. When Sennacherib heard the report, he sent messengers again to Hezekiah with a letter. It said, "Tell Hezekiah, the
king of Judah, 'Don't let the god you depend on trick you. He says,
"Jerusalem will not be handed over to the king of Assyria." But
don't believe him. I'm sure you have heard about what the kings of
Assyria have done to all the other countries. They have destroyed
them completely. So do you think you will be saved? The kings who
ruled before me destroyed many nations. Did the gods of those nations save them? Did the gods of Gozan, Harran or Rezeph save
them? What about the gods of the people of Eden who were in Tel
Assar? Where is the king of Hamath? Where is the king of Arpad?
Where are the kings of Lair, Sepharvaim, Hena and Ivvah?' "

When Hezekiah received the letter from the messengers, he
read it. Then he went up to the LORD's temple. There he spread
the letter out in front of the LORD. Hezekiah prayed to the LORD.
He said, "LORD who rules over all, you are the God of Israel. You sit
on your throne between the cherubim. You alone are God over all
the kingdoms on earth. You have made heaven and earth. Listen,
LORD. Hear us. Open your eyes, LORD. Look at the trouble we're in.
Listen to what Sennacherib is saying. You are the living God. And
he dares to make fun of you!

"LORD, it's true that the kings of Assyria have completely
destroyed many nations and their lands. LORD our God, save us
from the power of Sennacherib. Then all the kingdoms of the
earth will know that you are the only God."

Isaiah sent a message to Hezekiah. Isaiah said, "The LORD is the
God of Israel. He says, 'You have prayed to me about Sennacherib,
the king of Assyria. So here is the message the LORD has spoken
against him. The LORD is telling him,

" ' "You will not win the battle over Zion.
    Its people hate you and make fun of you.

The people of Jerusalem lift up their heads proudly
  as you run away.
Who have you laughed at?
  Who have you spoken evil things against?
  Who have you raised your voice against?
Who have you looked at so proudly?
  You have done it against me.
  I am the Holy One of Israel!

" ' "But I, the Lord, say, 'Haven't you heard what I have done?
  Long ago I arranged for you to do this.
In days of old I planned it.
  Now I have made it happen.
You have turned cities with high walls
  into piles of stone.
Their people do not have any power left.
  They are troubled and put to shame.

" ' " 'But I know where you are.
  I know when you come and go.
  I know how very angry you are with me.
You roar against me and brag.
  And I have heard your bragging.
So I will put my hook in your nose.
  I will put my bit in your mouth.
And I will make you go home
  by the same way you came.' " ' "

Then the angel of the Lord went into the camp of the Assyrians. He put to death 185,000 soldiers there. The people of Jerusalem got up the next morning. They looked out and saw all the dead bodies. So Sennacherib, the king of Assyria, took the army tents down. Then he left. He returned to Nineveh and stayed there.

One day Sennacherib was worshiping in the temple of his god Nisrok. His sons Adrammelek and Sharezer killed him with their swords.

In those days Hezekiah became very sick. He knew he was about to die. Isaiah went to see him. Isaiah was the son of Amoz. Isaiah told Hezekiah, "The Lord says, 'Put everything in order. Make out your will. You are going to die soon. You will not get well again.'"

Hezekiah turned his face toward the wall. He prayed to the Lord. He said, "Lord, please remember how faithful I've been to you. I've lived the way you wanted me to. I've served you with all my heart. I've done what is good in your sight." And Hezekiah wept bitterly.

A message from the Lord came to Isaiah. The Lord said, "Go and speak to Hezekiah. Tell him, 'The Lord, the God of King David, says, "I have heard your prayer. I have seen your tears. I will add 15 years to your life. And I will save you and this city from the power of the king of Assyria. I will guard this city.

Here is a song of praise that was written by Hezekiah, the king of Judah. He wrote it after he was sick and had gotten well again.

I said, "I'm enjoying the best years of my life.
    Must I now go through the gates of death?
    Will the rest of my years be taken away from me?"
I said, "Lord, I'll never see you again
    while I'm still alive.
I'll never see people anymore.
    I'll never again be with those who live in this world.

"But what can I say?
    You have promised to heal me.
    And you yourself have done it.
Once I was proud and bitter.
    But now I will live the rest of my life free of pride.
Lord, people find the will to live because you keep your
        promises.
    And my spirit also finds life in your promises.
You brought me back to health.
    You let me live.
I'm sure it was for my benefit
    that I suffered such great pain.
You love me. You kept me
    from going down into the pit of death.

You have put all my sins
   behind your back.
People in the grave can't praise you.
   Dead people can't sing praise to you.
Those who go down to the grave
   can't hope for you to be faithful to them.
It is those who are alive who praise you.
   And that's what I'm doing today.
Parents tell their children
   about how faithful you are.

Then Isaiah said to Hezekiah, "Listen to the message of the LORD who rules over all. He says, 'You can be sure the time will come when everything in your palace will be carried off to Babylon. Everything the kings before you have stored up until this day will be taken away. There will not be anything left,' says the LORD. 'Some of the members of your family line will be taken away. They will be your own flesh and blood. They will include the children who will be born into your family line. And they will serve the king of Babylon in his palace.'"

"The message the LORD has spoken through you is good," Hezekiah replied. He thought, "There will be peace and safety while I'm still living."

remember what you read

1. What is something you noticed for the first time?

_____

_____

_____

_____

2. What questions did you have?

_____

_____

_____

_____

3. Was there anything that bothered you?

_____

_____

_____

_____

4. What did you learn about loving God?

_____

_____

_____

_____

5. What did you learn about loving others?

_____

_____

_____

_____

introduction to Isaiah, part 6

Today's reading starts a very different part of the book of Isaiah's prophecy. It talks to God's people as they come back from living in Babylon. King Cyrus of Persia had decided to send everyone home. This section is about the people of Judah (also called Israel) being restored.

A new person is introduced: God's "servant." The servant is complicated. Sometimes he is the prophet. Sometimes he is the nation of Israel. Sometimes he is King Cyrus. On Day 12, you will read the servant is "willing to give his life as a sacrifice" and take "the sins of many on himself." Do you know who this might be talking about? The writers of the New Testament say that Jesus is the servant who did these things. Don't be confused by these different people. Enjoy the beauty of what God is doing to bring back his people.

∽∾∽

"Comfort my people," says your God.
   "Comfort them.
Speak tenderly to the people of Jerusalem.
   Announce to them
that their hard labor has been completed.
   Tell them that their sin has been paid for.
Tell them the LORD has punished them enough
   for all their sins."

A messenger is calling out,
"In the desert prepare
   the way for the LORD.

Make a straight road through it
  for our God.
Every valley will be filled in.
  Every mountain and hill will be made level.
The rough ground will be smoothed out.
  The rocky places will be made flat.
Then the glory of the LORD will appear.
  And everyone will see it together.
The LORD has spoken."

Another messenger says, "Cry out."
  And I said, "What should I cry?"

"Cry out, 'All people are like grass.
  They don't stay faithful to me any longer than wildflowers
    last.
The grass dries up. The flowers fall to the ground.
  That happens when the LORD makes his wind blow on them.
  So people are just like grass.
The grass dries up. The flowers fall to the ground.
  But what our God says will stand forever.'"

Zion, you are bringing good news to your people.
  Go up on a high mountain and announce it.
Jerusalem, you are bringing good news to them.
  Shout the message loudly.
Shout it out loud. Don't be afraid.
  Say to the towns of Judah,
  "Your God is coming!"
The LORD and King is coming with power.
  He rules with a powerful arm.
He has set his people free.
  He is bringing them back as his reward.
  He has won the battle over their enemies.
He takes care of his flock like a shepherd.
  He gathers the lambs in his arms.
He carries them close to his heart.
  He gently leads those that have little ones.

Who has measured the oceans by using the palm of his
    hand?
    Who has used the width of his hand to mark off the sky?
Who has measured out the dust of the earth in a basket?
    Who has weighed the mountains on scales?
    Who has weighed the hills in a balance?
Who can ever understand the Spirit of the LORD?
    Who can ever give him advice?
Did the LORD have to ask anyone to help him understand?
    Did he have to ask someone to teach him the right way?
Who taught him what he knows?
    Who showed him how to understand?

"So who will you compare me with?
    Who is equal to me?" says the Holy One.
Look up toward the sky.
    Who created everything you see?
The LORD causes the stars to come out at night one by one.
    He calls out each one of them by name.
His power and strength are great.
    So none of the stars is missing.

Family of Jacob, why do you complain,
    "The LORD doesn't notice our condition"?
People of Israel, why do you say,
    "Our God doesn't pay any attention to our rightful claims"?
Don't you know who made everything?
    Haven't you heard about him?
The LORD is the God who lives forever.
    He created everything on earth.
He won't become worn out or get tired.
    No one will ever know how great his understanding is.
He gives strength to those who are tired.
    He gives power to those who are weak.

Even young people become worn out and get tired.
    Even the best of them trip and fall.
But those who trust in the LORD
    will receive new strength.
They will fly as high as eagles.
    They will run and not get tired.
    They will walk and not grow weak.

⟳⟳⟳

"Here is my servant. I take good care of him.
    I have chosen him. I am very pleased with him.
I will put my Spirit on him.
    He will bring justice to the nations.
He will not shout or cry out.
    He will not raise his voice in the streets.
He will not break a bent twig.
    He will not put out a dimly burning flame.
He will be faithful and make everything right.
    He will not grow weak or lose hope.
He will not give up until he brings justice to the earth.
    The islands will put their hope in his teaching."

God created the heavens and stretches them out.
    The LORD spreads out the earth with everything that grows
        on it.
    He gives breath to its people.
He gives life to those who walk on it.
    He says to his servant,
"I, the LORD, have chosen you to do what is right.
    I will take hold of your hand.
I will keep you safe.
    You will put into effect my covenant with the people of
        Israel.
    And you will be a light for the Gentiles.
You will open eyes that can't see.
    You will set prisoners free.
    Those who sit in darkness will come out of their cells.

"I am the Lord. That is my name!
    I will not let any other god share my glory.
    I will not let statues of gods share my praise.
What I said would happen has taken place.
    Now I announce new things to you.
Before they even begin to happen,
    I announce them to you."

Sing a new song to the Lord.
    Sing praise to him from one end of the earth to the other.
Sing, you who sail out on the ocean.
    Sing, all you creatures in it.
Sing, you islands.
    Sing, all you who live there.
The Lord will march out like a mighty warrior.
    He will stir up his anger like a soldier getting ready to fight.
He will shout the battle cry.
    And he will win the battle over his enemies.

Long ago the Lord opened
    a way for his people to go through the Red Sea.
    He made a path through the mighty waters.
He caused Egypt to send out its chariots and horses.
    He sent its entire army to its death.
Its soldiers lay down there.
    They never got up again.
    They were destroyed.
They were blown out like a dimly burning flame.
    But the Lord says,
"Forget the things that happened in the past.
    Do not keep on thinking about them.
I am about to do something new.
    It is beginning to happen even now.
    Don't you see it coming?

I am going to make a way for you to go through the desert.
  I will make streams of water in the dry and empty land.
Even wild dogs and owls honor me.
  That is because I provide water in the desert
  for my people to drink.
I cause streams to flow in the dry and empty land
  for my chosen ones.
I do it for the people I made for myself.
  I want them to sing praise to me.

"Family of Jacob, listen to me. You are my servant.
  People of Israel, I have chosen you.
I made you. I formed you when you were born as a nation.
  I will help you.
  So listen to what I am saying.
Family of Jacob, do not be afraid. You are my servant.
  People of Israel, I have chosen you.
I will pour out water on the thirsty land.
  I will make streams flow on the dry ground.
I will pour out my Spirit on your children.
  I will pour out my blessing on their children after them.
They will spring up like grass in a meadow.
  They will grow like poplar trees near flowing streams.
Some will say, 'We belong to the Lord.'
  Others will call themselves by Jacob's name.
Still others will write on their hands,
  'We belong to the Lord.'
  And they will be called by the name of Israel.

"I am Israel's King. I set them free.
  I am the Lord who rules over all.
  So listen to what I am saying.
I am the first and the last.
  I am the one and only God.

People make statues of gods.
But those gods can't do any good.
A carpenter measures a piece of wood with a line.
He draws a pattern on it with a marker.
He cuts out a statue with sharp tools.
He marks it with compasses.
He shapes it into the form of a beautiful human being.
He does this so he can put it in a temple.
He cuts down a cedar tree.
Or perhaps he takes a cypress or an oak tree.
It might be a tree that grew in the forest.
Or it might be a pine tree he planted.
And the rain made it grow.
A man gets wood from trees to burn.
He uses some of it to warm himself.
He starts a fire and bakes bread.
But he also uses some of it to make a god and
worship it.
He makes a statue of a god and bows down to it.
He burns half of the wood in the fire.
He prepares a meal over it.
He cooks meat over it.
He eats until he is full.
He also warms himself. He says,
"Good! I'm getting warm.
The fire is nice and hot."
From the rest of the wood he makes a statue.
It becomes his god.
He bows down and worships it.
He prays to it. He says,
"Save me! You are my god!"
No one even stops to think about this.
No one has any sense or understanding.
If anyone did, they would say,
"I used half of the wood for fuel.
I even baked bread over the fire.
I cooked meat. Then I ate it.

Should I now make a statue of a god
  out of the wood that's left over?
Should I bow down to a block of wood?
  The Lord would hate that."
He can't save himself.
  He can't bring himself to say,
"This thing I'm holding in my right hand
  isn't really a god at all."

The Lord says, "Family of Jacob, remember these things.
  People of Israel, you are my servant.
I have made you. You are my servant.
  Israel, I will not forget you.
I will sweep your sins away as if they were a cloud.
  I will blow them away as if they were the morning mist.
Return to me.
  Then I will set you free."

Sing for joy, you heavens!
  The Lord does wonderful things.
Shout out loud, you earth!
  Burst into song, you mountains!
  Sing, you forests and all your trees!
The Lord sets the family of Jacob free.
  He shows his glory in Israel.

remember what you read

1. What is something you noticed for the first time?

_____

_____

_____

_____

2. What questions did you have?

_____

_____

_____

_____

3. Was there anything that bothered you?

_____

_____

_____

_____

4. What did you learn about loving God?

_____

_____

_____

_____

5. What did you learn about loving others?

_____

_____

_____

_____

introduction to Isaiah, part 7

Isaiah continues talking about God's people being restored and moving back to their homeland. He also keeps talking about God's servant. The servant helps bring back Israel, and Israel helps heal the world.

∽∾∾

The LORD says,
"People of Israel, I set you free.
I formed you when you were born as a nation.

"I am the LORD. I am the Maker of everything.
I alone stretch out the heavens.
I spread out the earth by myself.

"Some prophets are not really prophets at all.
I show that their signs are fake.
I make those who practice evil magic look foolish.
I destroy the learning of those who think they are wise.
Their knowledge does not make any sense at all.
I make the words of my servants the prophets come
true.
I carry out what my messengers say will happen.

"I say about Jerusalem,
'My people will live there again.'
I say about the towns of Judah,
'They will be rebuilt.'

I say about their broken-down buildings,
  'I will make them like new again.'
I say to the deep waters,
  'Dry up. Let your streams become dry.'
I say about Cyrus,
  'He is my shepherd.
  He will accomplish everything I want him to.
He will say about Jerusalem,
  "Let it be rebuilt."
And he will say about the temple,
  "Let its foundations be laid." '

"Cyrus is my anointed king.
  I take hold of his right hand.
I give him the power
  to bring nations under his control.
I help him strip kings of their power
  to go to war against him.
I break city gates open so he can go through them.
  I say to him,
'I will march out ahead of you.
  I will make the mountains level.
I will break down bronze gates.
  I will cut through their heavy iron bars.
I will give you treasures that are hidden away.
  I will give you riches that are stored up in secret places.
Then you will know that I am the LORD.
  I am the God of Israel.
  I am sending for you by name.
Cyrus, I am sending for you by name.
  I am doing it for the good of the family of Jacob.
  They are my servant.
I am doing it for Israel.
  They are my chosen people.
You do not know anything about me.
  But I am giving you a title of honor.
I am the LORD. There is no other LORD.
  I am the one and only God.

You do not know anything about me.
　　But I will make you strong.
Then people will know there is no God but me.
　　Everyone from where the sun rises in the east
　　to where it sets in the west will know it.
I am the LORD.
　　There is no other LORD.
I cause light to shine. I also create darkness.
　　I bring good times. I also create hard times.
　　I do all these things. I am the LORD.

I will stir up Cyrus and help him win his battles.
　　I will make all his roads straight.
He will rebuild Jerusalem.
　　My people have been taken away from their country.
　　But he will set them free.
I will not pay him to do it.
　　He will not receive a reward for it,"
　　says the LORD who rules over all.

The LORD created the heavens.
　　He is God.
He formed the earth and made it.
　　He set it firmly in place.
He didn't create it to be empty.
　　Instead, he formed it for people to live on.
He says, "I am the LORD.
　　There is no other LORD.
I have not spoken in secret.
　　I have not spoken from a dark place.
I have not said to Jacob's people,
　　'It is useless to look for me.'
I am the LORD. I always speak the truth.
　　I always say what is right.

"All you who live anywhere on earth,
　　turn to me and be saved.
　　I am God. There is no other God.

I have made a promise in my own name.
  I have spoken with complete honesty.
  I will not take back a single word. I said,
'Everyone will kneel down to me.
  Everyone's mouth will make promises in my name.'
They will say, 'The Lord is the only one who can save us.
  Only he can make us strong.' "
All those who have been angry with the Lord will come to
    him.
  And they will be put to shame.
But the Lord will save all the people of Israel.
  And so they will boast about the Lord.

The Lord says, "Queen city of the Babylonians,
  go into a dark prison. Sit there quietly.
You will not be called
  the queen of kingdoms anymore.
I was angry with my people.
  I treated them as if they did not belong to me.
I handed them over to you.
  And you did not show them any pity.
You even placed heavy loads on their old people.
  You said, 'I am queen forever!'
But you did not think about what you were doing.
  You did not consider how things might turn out.

"So listen, you who love pleasure.
  You think you are safe and secure.
You say to yourself,
  'I am like a god.
  No one is greater than I am.
I'll never be a widow.
  And my children will never be taken away from me.'
But both of these things will happen to you in a moment.
  They will take place on a single day.

You will lose your children.
  And you will become a widow.
That is what will happen to you.
  All your evil magic
  and powerful spells will not save you.
You have felt secure in your evil ways.
  You have said, 'No one sees what I'm doing.'
Your wisdom and knowledge lead you astray.
  You say to yourself,
  'I am like a god. No one is greater than I am.'
So horrible trouble will come on you.
  You will not know how to use your evil magic to make it go
    away.
Great trouble will fall on you.
  No amount of money can keep it away.
Something terrible will happen to you all at once.
  You will not see it coming ahead of time.

☙

"Family of Jacob, listen to me.
  People of Israel, pay attention.
  I have chosen you.
I am the first and the last.
  I am the LORD.
With my own hand I laid the foundations of the earth.
  With my right hand I spread out the heavens.
When I send for them,
  they come and stand ready to obey me.

"People of Israel, come together and listen to me.
  What other god has said ahead of time that certain things
    would happen?
I have chosen Cyrus.
  He will carry out my plans against Babylon.
  He will use his power against the Babylonians.
I myself have spoken.
  I have chosen him to carry out my purpose.

I will bring him to Babylon.
  He will succeed in what I tell him to do.

"Come close and listen to me.

"From the first time I said Cyrus was coming,
  I did not do it in secret.
  When he comes, I will be there."

The Lord and King has filled me with his Spirit.
  People of Israel, he has sent me to you.

The Lord is the Holy One of Israel.
  He sets his people free. He says to them,
"I am the Lord your God.
  I teach you what is best for you.
  I direct you in the way you should go.
I wish you would pay attention to my commands.
  If you did, peace would flow over you like a river.
  Godliness would sweep over you like the waves of the ocean.
Your family would be like the sand.
  Your children after you would be as many as the grains of
    sand by the sea.
  It would be impossible to count them.
I would always accept the members of your family line.
  They would never disappear or be destroyed."

People of Israel, leave Babylon!
  Hurry up and get away from the Babylonians!
Here is what I want you to announce.
  Make it known with shouts of joy.
Send the news out from one end of the earth to the other.
  Say, "The Lord has set free his servant Jacob."
They didn't get thirsty when he led them through the
    deserts.
  He made water flow out of the rock for them.
He broke the rock open,
  and water came out of it.

"There is no peace for those who are evil," says the Lord.

Before I was born the Lord chose me to serve him.
  Before I was born the Lord spoke my name.
He made my words like a sharp sword.
  He hid me in the palm of his hand.
He made me into a sharpened arrow.
  He took good care of me and kept me safe.
He said to me, "You are my true servant Israel.
  I will show my glory through you."
But I said, "In spite of my hard work,
  I feel as if I haven't accomplished anything.
I've used up all my strength.
  It seems as if everything I've done is worthless.
But the Lord will give me what I should receive.
  My God will reward me."

The Lord formed me in my mother's body to be his servant.
  He wanted me to bring the family of Jacob back to him.
He wanted me to gather the people of Israel to himself.
  The Lord will honor me.
  My God will give me strength.

Here is what the Lord says to me.

"It is not enough for you as my servant
  to bring the tribes of Jacob back to their land.
It is not enough for you to bring back
  the people of Israel I have kept alive.
I will also make you a light for the Gentiles.
  Then you will make it possible for the whole world to be
    saved."

The Lord says to his servant,

"When it is time to have mercy on you, I will answer your
    prayers.
  When it is time to save you, I will help you.

I will keep you safe.
　You will put into effect my covenant with the people of
　　Israel.
Then their land will be made like new again.
　Each tribe will be sent back to its territory that was left
　　empty.
I want you to say to the prisoners, 'Come out.'
　Tell those who are in their dark cells, 'You are free!'

"On their way home they will eat beside the roads.
　They will find plenty to eat on every bare hill.
They will not get hungry or thirsty.
　The heat from the desert sun will not beat down on them.
The God who has tender love for them will guide them.
　Like a shepherd, he will lead them beside springs of water.
I will make roads across the mountains.
　I will build wide roads for my people.
They will come from far away.
　Some of them will come from the north.
Others will come from the west.
　Still others will come from Aswan in the south."

Shout for joy, you heavens!
　Be glad, you earth!
　Burst into song, you mountains!
The Lord will comfort his people.
　He will show his tender love to those who are suffering.

remember what you read

1. What is something you noticed for the first time?

_____

_____

_____

_____

2. What questions did you have?

_____

_____

_____

_____

3. Was there anything that bothered you?

_____

_____

_____

_____

4. What did you learn about loving God?

_____

_____

_____

_____

5. What did you learn about loving others?

_____

_____

_____

_____

ISAIAH, PART 8

introduction to Isaiah, part 8

Isaiah continues talking about God's people being restored and moving back to their homeland. He also keeps talking about God's servant. The servant helps bring back Israel, and Israel helps heal the world.

The LORD says, "Listen to me, you who want to do what is
    right.
  Pay attention, you who look to me.
Consider the rock you were cut out of.
  Think about the rock pit you were dug from.
Consider Abraham. He is the father of your people.
  Think about Sarah. She is your mother.
When I chose Abraham, he did not have any children.
  But I blessed him and gave him many of them.
You can be sure that I will comfort Zion's people.
  I will look with loving concern on all their destroyed
    buildings.
I will make their deserts like Eden.
  I will make their dry and empty land like the garden of the
    LORD.
Joy and gladness will be there.
  People will sing and give thanks to me.

"Listen to me, my people.
  Pay attention, my nation.

My instruction will go out to the nations.
  I make everything right.
  That will be a guiding light for them.
The time for me to set you free is near.
  I will soon save you.
  My powerful arm will make everything right among the
    nations.

ഝ

Wake up, arm of the LORD! Wake up!
  Dress yourself with strength as if it were your clothes!
Wake up, just as you did in the past.
  Wake up, as you did long ago.
Didn't you cut Rahab to pieces?
  Didn't you stab that sea monster to death?
Didn't you dry up the Red Sea?
  Didn't you dry up those deep waters?
You made a road on the bottom of that sea.
  Then those who were set free went across.
Those the LORD has saved will return to their land.
  They will sing as they enter the city of Zion.
  Joy that lasts forever will be like beautiful crowns on their
    heads.
They will be filled with gladness and joy.
  Sorrow and sighing will be gone.

The LORD says to his people,
  "I comfort you because of who I am.
Why are you afraid of mere human beings?
  They are like grass that dries up.
How can you forget me? I made you.
  I stretch out the heavens.
  I lay the foundations of the earth.
Why are you terrified every day?
  Is it because those who are angry with you are crushing
    you?
  Is it because they are trying to destroy you?

Their anger can't harm you anymore.
  You prisoners who are so afraid will soon be set free.
You will not die in your prison cells.
  You will not go without food.
I am the LORD your God.
  I stir up the ocean. I make its waves roar.
  My name is the LORD Who Rules Over All.
I have put my words in your mouth.
  I have kept you safe in the palm of my hand.
I set the heavens in place.
  I laid the foundations of the earth.
  I say to Zion, 'You are my people.' "

Wake up! Zion, wake up!
  Dress yourself with strength as if it were your clothes.
Holy city of Jerusalem,
  put on your clothes of glory.
Those who haven't been circumcised will never enter you
    again.
  Neither will those who are "unclean."
Get up, Jerusalem! Shake off your dust.
  Take your place on your throne.
Captured people of Zion,
  remove the chains from your neck.

What a beautiful sight it is
  to see messengers coming with good news!
How beautiful to see them coming down from the mountains
  with a message about peace!
How wonderful it is when they bring the good news
  that we are saved!
How wonderful when they say to Zion,
  "Your God rules!"
Listen! Those on guard duty are shouting out the message.
  With their own eyes

they see the LORD returning to Zion.
  So they shout for joy.
Burst into songs of joy together,
  you broken-down buildings in Jerusalem.
The LORD has comforted his people.
  He has set Jerusalem free.
The LORD will use the power of his holy arm to save his
      people.
  All the nations will see him do it.
  Everyone from one end of the earth to the other will see it.

ممم

The LORD says, "My servant will act wisely and accomplish
      his task.
  He will be highly honored. He will be greatly respected.
Many people were shocked when they saw him.
  He was so scarred that he no longer looked like a person.
  His body was so twisted that he did not look like a human
      being anymore.
But many nations will be surprised when they see what he
      has done.
  Kings will be so amazed that they will not be able to say
      anything.
They will understand things they were never told.
  They will know the meaning of things they never heard."

Who has believed what we've been saying?
  Who has seen the LORD's saving power?
His servant grew up like a tender young plant.
  He grew like a root coming up out of dry ground.
He didn't have any beauty or majesty that made us notice
      him.
  There wasn't anything special about the way he looked that
      drew us to him.
People looked down on him. They didn't accept him.
  He knew all about pain and suffering.

He was like someone people turn their faces away from.
　　We looked down on him. We didn't have any respect for
　　　him.

He suffered the things we should have suffered.
　　He took on himself the pain that should have been ours.
But we thought God was punishing him.
　　We thought God was wounding him and making him
　　　suffer.
But the servant was pierced because we had sinned.
　　He was crushed because we had done what was evil.
He was punished to make us whole again.
　　His wounds have healed us.
All of us are like sheep. We have wandered away from
　　　God.
　　All of us have turned to our own way.
And the Lord has placed on his servant
　　the sins of all of us.

He was treated badly and made to suffer.
　　But he didn't open his mouth.
He was led away like a lamb to be killed.
　　Sheep are silent while their wool is being cut off.
　　In the same way, he didn't open his mouth.
He was arrested and sentenced to death.
　　Then he was taken away.
　　He was cut off from this life.
He was punished for the sins of my people.
　　Who among those who were living at that time
　　tried to stop what was happening?
He was given a grave with those who were evil.
　　But his body was buried in the tomb of a rich man.
He was killed even though he hadn't harmed anyone.
　　And he had never lied to anyone.

The Lord says, "It was my plan to crush him
　　and cause him to suffer.
　　　I made his life an offering to pay for sin.

But he will see all his children after him.
In fact, he will continue to live.
My plan will be brought about through him.
After he has suffered, he will see the light of life.
And he will be satisfied.
My godly servant will make many people godly
because of what he will accomplish.
He will be punished for their sins.
So I will give him a place of honor among those who are
great.
He will be rewarded just like others who win the battle.
That's because he was willing to give his life as a sacrifice.
He was counted among those who had committed crimes.
He took the sins of many people on himself.
And he gave his life for those who had done what is wrong."

~~~

"Jerusalem, sing!
You are now like a woman who never had a child.
Burst into song! Shout for joy!
You who have never had labor pains,
you are now all alone.
But you will have more children than a woman who still
has a husband,"
says the Lord.

"Suffering city, you have been beaten by storms.
You have not been comforted.
I will rebuild you with turquoise stones.
I will rebuild your foundations with lapis lazuli.
I will line the top of your city wall with rubies.
I will make your gates out of gleaming jewels.
And I will make all your walls out of precious stones.
I will teach all your children.
And they will enjoy great peace.
When you do what is right,
you will be made secure.

Your leaders will not be mean to you.
    You will not have anything to be afraid of.
You will not be terrified anymore.
    Terror will not come near you.
People might attack you. But I will not be the cause of it.
    Those who attack you will give themselves up to you.

⁓◦⦉⦉◦⁓

"Come, all you who are thirsty.
    Come and drink the water I offer to you.
You who do not have any money, come.
    Buy and eat the grain I give you.
Come and buy wine and milk.
    You will not have to pay anything for it.
Why spend money on what is not food?
    Why work for what does not satisfy you?
Listen carefully to me.
    Then you will eat what is good.
    You will enjoy the richest food there is.
Listen and come to me.
    Pay attention to me.
    Then you will live.
I will make a covenant with you that will last forever.
    I will give you my faithful love.
    I promised it to David.
I made him a witness to the nations.
    He became a ruler and commander over them.
You too will send for nations you do not know.
    Even though you do not know them,
    they will come running to you.
That is what I will do. I am the Lord your God.
    I am the Holy One of Israel.
    I have honored you."

Turn to the Lord before it's too late.
    Call out to him while he's still ready to help you.

Let those who are evil stop doing evil things.
    And let them quit thinking evil thoughts.
Let them turn to the LORD.
    The LORD will show them his tender love.
Let them turn to our God.
    He is always ready to forgive.

"My thoughts are not like your thoughts.
    And your ways are not like my ways,"
    announces the LORD.
"The heavens are higher than the earth.
    And my ways are higher than your ways.
    My thoughts are higher than your thoughts.
The rain and the snow
    come down from the sky.
They do not return to it
    without watering the earth.
They make plants come up and grow.
    The plants produce seeds for farmers.
    They also produce food for people to eat.
The words I speak are like that.
    They will not return to me without producing results.
They will accomplish what I want them to.
    They will do exactly what I sent them to do.

"My people, you will go out of Babylon with joy.
    You will be led out of it in peace.
The mountains and hills
    will burst into song as you go.
And all the trees in the fields
    will clap their hands.
Juniper trees will grow where there used to be bushes that
        had thorns on them.
    And myrtle trees will grow where there used to be thorns.
That will bring me great fame.
    It will be a lasting reminder of what I can do.
    It will stand forever."

remember what you read

1. What is something you noticed for the first time?

_____

_____

_____

_____

2. What questions did you have?

_____

_____

_____

_____

3. Was there anything that bothered you?

_____

_____

_____

_____

4. What did you learn about loving God?

_____

_____

_____

_____

5. What did you learn about loving others?

_____

_____

_____

_____

introduction to Isaiah, part 9

The people of Judah are back in their homeland. They feel hurt and scared by God's perfect and right judgment. So Isaiah continues to tell them that they can trust their God. He also reminds them it is foolish to worship statues of gods. Everything will be good and right if they trust God.

The LORD says,

"Do what is fair and right.
    I will soon come and save you.
    Soon everyone will know that what I do is right.
Blessed is the person who does what I want them to.
    They are faithful in keeping the Sabbath day.
They do not misuse it.
    They do not do what is evil on that day."

Suppose an outsider wants to follow the LORD.
    Then that person shouldn't say,
    "The LORD won't accept me as one of his people."
And a eunuch shouldn't say,
    "I'm like a dry tree
    that doesn't bear any fruit."

The LORD says,

"Suppose some eunuchs keep my Sabbath days.
    They choose to do what pleases me.
    And they are faithful in keeping my covenant.

Then I will set up a monument in the area of my temple.
   Their names will be written on it.
   That will be better for them than having sons and
      daughters.
The names of the eunuchs will be remembered forever.
   They will never be forgotten.

"Suppose outsiders want to follow me
   and serve me.
They want to love me
   and worship me.
They keep the Sabbath day and do not misuse it.
   And they are faithful in keeping my covenant.
Then I will bring them to my holy mountain of Zion.
   I will give them joy in my house.
They can pray there.
   I will accept their burnt offerings and sacrifices on my altar.
My house will be called
   a house where people from all nations can pray."
The LORD and King will gather
   those who were taken away from their homes in Israel.
He announces, "I will gather them to myself.
   And I will gather others to join them."

⚬⚬⚬⚬

A messenger says,

"Build up the road! Build it up! Get it ready!
   Remove anything that would keep my people from coming
      back."
The God who is highly honored lives forever.
   His name is holy. He says,
"I live in a high and holy place.
   But I also live with anyone who turns away from their sins.
   I live with anyone who is not proud.
I give new life to them.
   I give it to anyone who turns away from their sins.

I will not find fault with my people forever.
  I will not always be angry with them.
If I were, I would cause their spirits to grow weak.
  The people I created would faint away.
I was very angry with them.
  They always longed for more and more of everything.
So I punished them for that sin.
  I turned my face away from them because I was angry.
  But they kept on wanting their own way.
I have seen what they have done.
  But I will heal them.
I will guide them.
    I will give those who mourn in Israel the comfort they had
      before.
    Then they will praise me.
I will give perfect peace to those who are far away and those
      who are near.
    And I will heal them," says the Lord.
But those who are evil are like the rolling sea.
  It never rests.
  Its waves toss up mud and sand.

"There is no peace for those who are evil," says my God.

⁓ᴓᴓᴓᴓ⁓

The Lord told me,

"Shout out loud. Do not hold back.
  Raise your voice like a trumpet.
Tell my people that they have refused to obey me.
  Tell the family of Jacob how much they have sinned.
Day after day they worship me.
    They seem ready and willing to know how I want them to
      live.
They act as if they were a nation that does what is right.
    They act as if they have not turned away from my
      commands.

They claim to want me to give them fair decisions.
They seem ready and willing to come near and worship me.
'We have gone without food,' they say.
'Why haven't you noticed it?
We have made ourselves suffer.
Why haven't you paid any attention to us?'

"On the day when you fast, you do as you please.
You take advantage of all your workers.
When you fast, it ends in arguing and fighting.
You hit one another with your fists.
That is an evil thing to do.
The way you are now fasting
keeps your prayers from being heard in heaven.
Do you think that is the way I want you to fast?
Is it only a time for people to make themselves suffer?
Is it only for people to bow their heads like tall grass bent by
the wind?
Is it only for people to lie down in ashes and clothes of
mourning?
Is that what you call a fast?
Do you think I can accept that?

"Here is the way I want you to fast.

"Set free those who are held by chains without any reason.
Untie the ropes that hold people as slaves.
Set free those who are crushed.
Break every evil chain.
Share your food with hungry people.
Provide homeless people with a place to stay.
Give naked people clothes to wear.
Provide for the needs of your own family.
Then the light of my blessing will shine on you like the rising
sun.
I will heal you quickly.
I will march out ahead of you.
And my glory will follow behind you and guard you.
That's because I always do what is right.

You will call out to me for help.
    And I will answer you.
You will cry out.
    And I will say, 'Here I am.'

"Get rid of the chains you use to hold others down.
    Stop pointing your finger at others as if they had done
        something wrong.
    Stop saying harmful things about them.
Work hard to feed hungry people.
    Satisfy the needs of those who are crushed.
Then my blessing will light up your darkness.
    And the night of your suffering will become as bright as the
        noonday sun.
I will always guide you.
    I will satisfy your needs in a land baked by the sun.
    I will make you stronger.
You will be like a garden that has plenty of water.
    You will be like a spring whose water never runs dry.
Your people will rebuild the cities that were destroyed long ago.
    And you will build again on the old foundations.
You will be called One Who Repairs Broken Walls.
    You will be called One Who Makes City Streets Like New
        Again.

"Do not work on the Sabbath day.
    Do not do just anything you want to on my holy day.
Make the Sabbath a day you can enjoy.
    Honor the Lord's holy day.
Do not work on it.
    Do not do just anything you want to.
    Do not talk about things that are worthless.
Then you will find your joy in me.
    I will give you control over the most important places in the
        land.
And you will enjoy all the good things
    in the land I gave your father Jacob."
The Lord has spoken.

The LORD sees that people aren't treating others fairly.
    That makes him unhappy.
He sees that there is no one who helps his people.
    He is shocked that no one stands up for them.
So he will use his own powerful arm to save them.
    He has the strength to do it because he is holy.
He will put the armor of holiness on his chest.
    He'll put the helmet of salvation on his head.
He'll pay people back for the wrong things they do.
    He'll wrap himself in anger as if it were a coat.
He will pay his enemies back for what they have done.
    He'll pour his anger out on them.
He'll punish those who attack him.
    He'll give the people in the islands what they have coming
        to them.
People in the west will show respect for the LORD's name.
    People in the east will worship him because of his glory.
The LORD will come like a rushing river that was held back.
    His breath will drive it along.

"I set my people free. I will come to Mount Zion.
    I will come to those in Jacob's family who turn away from
        their sins,"
announces the LORD.

"Here is the covenant I will make with them," says the LORD. "My Spirit is on you and will not leave you. I have put my words in your mouth. They will never leave your mouth. And they will never leave the mouths of your children or their children after them. That will be true for all time to come," says the LORD.

The Spirit of the LORD and King is on me.
    The LORD has anointed me
        to announce good news to poor people.

He has sent me to comfort
    those whose hearts have been broken.
He has sent me to announce freedom
    for those who have been captured.
He wants me to set prisoners free
    from their dark cells.
He has sent me to announce the year
    when he will set his people free.
He wants me to announce the day
    when he will pay his enemies back.
Our God has sent me to comfort all those who are sad.
    He wants me to help those in Zion who are filled with
        sorrow.
I will put beautiful crowns on their heads
    in place of ashes.
I will anoint them with olive oil to give them joy
    instead of sorrow.
I will give them a spirit of praise
    in place of a spirit of sadness.
They will be like oak trees that are strong and straight.
    The Lord himself will plant them in the land.
    That will show how glorious he is.

They will rebuild the places that were destroyed long ago.
    They will repair the buildings that have been broken down
        for many years.
They will make the destroyed cities like new again.
    They have been broken down for a very long time.
Outsiders will serve you by taking care of your flocks.
    People from other lands will work in your fields and
        vineyards.
You will be called priests of the Lord.
    You will be named workers for our God.
You will enjoy the wealth of nations.
    You will brag about getting their riches.

The Lord says, "I love those who do what is right.
    I hate it when people steal and do other sinful things.

So I will be faithful to my people.
    And I will bless them.
I will make a covenant with them
    that will last forever.
Their children after them will be famous among the nations.
    Their families will be praised by people everywhere.
All those who see them will agree
    that I have blessed them."

The people of Jerusalem will say,
    "We take great delight in the LORD.
    We are joyful because we belong to our God.
He has dressed us with salvation as if it were our clothes.
    He has put robes of godliness on us.
We are like a groom who is dressed up for his wedding.
    We are like a bride who decorates herself with her jewels.
The soil makes the young plant come up.
    A garden causes seeds to grow.
In the same way, the LORD and King will make godliness grow.
    And all the nations will praise him."

remember what you read

1. What is something you noticed for the first time?

_____

_____

_____

_____

2. What questions did you have?

_____

_____

_____

_____

3. Was there anything that bothered you?

_____

_____

_____

_____

4. What did you learn about loving God?

_____

_____

_____

_____

5. What did you learn about loving others?

_____

_____

_____

_____

ISAIAH, PART 10

introduction to Isaiah, part 10

This is the final reading in Isaiah. He is talking to Judah, who is back in the homeland after exile in Babylon. Isaiah says whatever has happened to Israel and Judah will happen to all nations and all creation. Those who obey God will live joyfully in a new creation. Those who disobey will be destroyed.

The LORD says, "For the good of Zion I will not keep
    silent.
  For Jerusalem's benefit I will not remain quiet.
I will not keep silent until what I will do for them
    shines like the sunrise.
I will not remain quiet until they are saved
    and shine like a blazing torch.
Jerusalem, the nations will see
    that I have made everything right for you.
    All their kings will see your glory.
You will be called by a new name.
    I myself will give it to you.
You will be like a glorious crown in my strong hand.
    You will be like a royal crown in my powerful hand.
People will not call you Deserted anymore.
    They will no longer name your land Empty.

Go out through your gates, people of Jerusalem! Go out!
    Prepare the way for the rest of your people to return

Build up the road! Build it up!
　　Remove the stones.
Raise a banner over the city
　　for the nations to see.

The Lord has announced a message
　　from one end of the earth to the other.
He has said, "Tell the people of Zion,
　　'Look! Your Savior is coming!
He is bringing his people back as his reward.
　　He has won the battle over their enemies.'"
They will be called the Holy People.
　　They will be called the People the Lord Set Free.
And Jerusalem will be named the City the Lord Cares About.
　　It will be named the City No Longer Deserted.

I will talk about the kind things the Lord has done.
　　I'll praise him for everything he's done for us.
He has done many good things
　　for the nation of Israel.
　　That's because he loves us and is very kind to us.
In the past he said, "They are my people.
　　They are children who will be faithful to me."
　　So he saved them.
When they suffered, he suffered with them.
　　He sent his angel to save them.
He set them free because he is loving and kind.
　　He lifted them up and carried them.
　　He did it again and again in days long ago.
But they refused to obey him.
　　They made his Holy Spirit sad.
So he turned against them and became their enemy.
　　He himself fought against them.

Then his people remembered what he did long ago.
　　They recalled the days of Moses and his people.

They asked, "Where is the God who brought
   Israel through the Red Sea?
   Moses led them as the shepherd of his flock.
Where is the God who put
   his Holy Spirit among them?
He used his glorious and powerful arm
   to help Moses.
He parted the waters of the sea in front of them.
   That mighty act made him famous forever.
   He led them through that deep sea.
Like a horse in open country,
   they didn't trip and fall.
They were like cattle that are taken down to the plains.
   They were given rest by the Spirit of the LORD."
That's how he guided his people.
   So he made a glorious name for himself.

LORD, look down from heaven.
   Look down from your holy and glorious throne.
Where is your great love for us?
   Where is your power?
Why don't you show us
   your tender love and concern?
You are our Father.
   Abraham might not accept us as his children.
   Jacob might not recognize us as his family.
But you are our Father, LORD.
   Your name is One Who Always Sets Us Free.

I wish you would open up your heavens
   and come down to us!
I wish the mountains would tremble
   when you show your power!
Long ago you did some wonderful things we didn't expect.
   You came down, and the mountains trembled
   when you showed your power.
No one's ears have ever heard of a God like you.
   No one's eyes have ever seen a God who is greater than you.

No God but you acts for the good
of those who trust in him.
You come to help those who enjoy doing what is right.
You help those who thank you for teaching them how to
live.
But when we continued to disobey you,
you became angry with us.
So how can we be saved?
All of us have become like someone who is "unclean."
All the good things we do are like dirty rags to you.
All of us are like leaves that have dried up.
Our sins sweep us away like the wind.
No one prays to you.
No one asks you for help.
You have turned your face away from us.
You have let us feel the effects of our sins.

LORD, you are our Father.
We are the clay. You are the potter.
Your hands made all of us.
Don't be so angry with us, LORD.
Don't remember our sins anymore.
Please have mercy on us.
All of us belong to you.

ळ

The LORD says, "I made myself known to those who were not
asking for me.
I was found by those who were not trying to find me.
I spoke to a nation that did not pray to me.
'Here I am,' I said. 'Here I am.'
All day long I have held out my hands
to welcome a stubborn nation.
They lead sinful lives.
They go where their evil thoughts take them.
They are always making me very angry.
They do it right in front of me.

So I will make sure they are fully punished
   for all the sins they have committed."

The LORD says,

"Sometimes juice is still left in grapes that have been
      crushed.
   So people say, 'Don't destroy them.
   They are still of some benefit.'
That is what I will do for the good of those who serve me.
   I will not destroy all my people.
I will give children
   to the families of Jacob and Judah.
   They will possess my entire land.
My chosen people will be given all of it.
   Those who serve me will live there.
Their flocks will eat in the rich grasslands of Sharon.
   Their herds will rest in the Valley of Achor.
   That is what I will do for my people who follow me.

∽∽∽

"I will create new heavens and a new earth.
   The things that have happened before will not be
      remembered.
   They will not even enter your minds.
So be glad and full of joy forever
   because of what I will create.
I will cause others to take delight in Jerusalem.
   They will be filled with joy
   when they see its people.
And I will be full of joy because of Jerusalem.
   I will take delight in my people.
Weeping and crying
   will not be heard there anymore.

"Babies in Jerusalem will no longer
   live only a few days.

Old people will not fail
  to live for a very long time.
Those who live to the age of 100
  will be thought of as mere children when they die.
Those who die before they are 100
  will be considered as having been under God's curse.
My people will build houses and live in them.
  They will plant vineyards and eat their fruit.
They will no longer build houses
  only to have others live in them.
They will no longer plant crops
  only to have others eat them.
My people will live to be as old as trees.
  My chosen ones will enjoy for a long time
  the things they have worked for.
Their work will not be worthless anymore.
  They will not have children who are sure to face sudden
    terror.
Instead, I will bless them.
  I will also bless their children after them.
Even before they call out to me, I will answer them.
  While they are still speaking, I will hear them.
Wolves and lambs will eat together.
  Lions will eat straw like oxen.
  Serpents will eat nothing but dust.
None of those animals will harm or destroy
  anything or anyone on my holy mountain of Zion,"
  says the LORD.

ℛℛℛ

The LORD says,

"Heaven is my throne.
  The earth is under my control.
So how could you ever build a house for me?
  Where would my resting place be?

Didn't I make everything by my power?
  That is how all things were created,"
  announces the LORD.

"The people I value are not proud.
  They are sorry for the wrong things they have done.
  They have great respect for what I say.
But others are not like that.
  They sacrifice bulls to me,
  but at the same time they kill people.
They offer lambs to me,
  but they also sacrifice dogs to other gods.
They bring grain offerings to me,
  but they also offer pig's blood to other gods.
They burn incense to me,
  but they also worship statues of gods.
They have chosen to go their own way.
  They take delight in things I hate.
So I have also made a choice.
  I will make them suffer greatly.
  I will bring on them what they are afraid of.
When I called out to them, no one answered me.
  When I spoke to them, no one listened.
They did what is evil in my sight.
  They chose to do what displeases me."

Listen to the word of the LORD.
  Listen, you who tremble with fear when he speaks. He says,
  "Some of your own people hate you.
  They turn their backs on you because you are faithful to
      me.
  They make fun of you and say,
'Let the LORD show his glory by saving you.
  Then we can see how happy you are.'
  But they will be put to shame.

"Be glad along with Jerusalem, all you who love her.
  Be filled with joy because of her.

Take great delight in her,
    all you who mourn over her.

"I will cause peace to flow over her like a river.
    I will make the wealth of nations sweep over her like a
        flooding stream.
You will nurse and be carried in her arms.
    You will play on her lap.
As a mother comforts her child,
    I will comfort you.
    You will find comfort in Jerusalem."

"Some people have planned to do many evil things. And they have carried out their plans. So I will come and gather the people of every nation and language. They will see my glory when I act.

"I will give them a sign. I will send to the nations some of those who are left alive. The people who live there have not heard about my fame. They have not seen my glory. But when I act, those I send will tell the nations about my glory. And they will bring back all the people of Israel from all those nations. They will bring them to my holy mountain in Jerusalem. My people will ride on horses, mules and camels. They will come in chariots and wagons," says the Lord. "Those messengers will bring my people as an offering to me. They will bring them to my temple, just as the Israelites bring their grain offerings in bowls that are 'clean.' And I will choose some of them to be priests and Levites," says the Lord.

"I will make new heavens and a new earth. And they will last forever," announces the Lord. "In the same way, your name and your children after you will last forever. Everyone will come and bow down to me. They will do it at every New Moon feast and on every Sabbath day," says the Lord. "When they go out of Jerusalem, they will see the dead bodies of those who refused to obey me. The worms that eat their bodies will not die. The fire that burns them will not be put out. It will make everyone sick just to look at them."

remember what you read

1. What is something you noticed for the first time?

_____

_____

_____

_____

2. What questions did you have?

_____

_____

_____

_____

3. Was there anything that bothered you?

_____

_____

_____

_____

4. What did you learn about loving God?

_____

_____

_____

_____

5. What did you learn about loving others?

_____

_____

_____

_____

ZEPHANIAH, NAHUM, HABAKKUK

introduction to Zephaniah

Zephaniah was likely the great-great-grandson of King Hezekiah. Hezekiah made many changes so the people of Judah could be faithful to their covenant agreement with God. But Hezekiah's son Manasseh was Judah's most evil king. So Zephaniah spoke God's words to Manasseh's grandson, Hezekiah's great-grandson, King Josiah. Josiah obeyed the covenant even better than Hezekiah. But Zephaniah knew Judah would still make bad choices. He warned that God would judge them. He also warned other nations of coming judgment. Like Isaiah, Zephaniah promised that a small group of people would return to Jerusalem.

The LORD spoke to Zephaniah during the rule of Josiah.

"I will sweep away everything
 from the face of the earth,"
 announces the LORD.
"I will destroy people and animals alike.
 I will wipe out the birds in the sky
 and the fish in the waters.
I will destroy the statues of gods that cause evil people to sin.
 That will happen when I destroy all human beings on the
  face of the earth,"
 announces the LORD.
"I will reach out my powerful hand against Judah.
 I will punish all those who live in Jerusalem.

I will destroy from this place
   what is left of Baal worship.

"At that time I will search Jerusalem with lamps.
   I will punish those who are so contented.
   They are like wine that has not been shaken up.
They think, 'The Lord won't do anything.
   He won't do anything good or bad.'
Their wealth will be stolen.
   Their houses will be destroyed.
The great day of the Lord is near.
   In fact, it is coming quickly.
The cries on that day are bitter.
   The Mighty Warrior shouts his battle cry.
At that time I will pour out my anger.
   There will be great suffering and pain.
It will be a day of horrible trouble.
   It will be a time of darkness and gloom.
   It will be filled with the blackest clouds.
Their silver and gold
   won't save them
   on the day the Lord pours out his anger.
The whole earth will be burned up
   when his jealous anger blazes out.
Everyone who lives on earth
   will come to a sudden end."

∽❦∾

Gather together,
   you shameful nation of Judah!
   Gather yourselves together!
Soon the Lord's great anger will come against you.
   The day of his wrath will come against you.
So look to him, all you people in the land
   who worship him faithfully.
   You always do what he commands you to do.

Continue to do what is right.
  Don't be proud.
Then perhaps the Lord will keep you safe
  on the day he pours out his anger on the world.

Philistia, the Lord has spoken against you.
  What happened to Canaan will happen to you.

The Lord says, "I will destroy you.
  No one will be left."

The Lord says,

"I have heard Moab make fun of my people.
  The Ammonites also laughed at them.
They told them that bad things
  would happen to their land.
So Moab will become like Sodom,"
  announces the Lord who rules over all.
  "Ammon will be like Gomorrah.
Weeds and salt pits will cover those countries.
  They will be dry and empty deserts forever.
Those who are still left alive among my people
  will take all their valuable things.
  So they will receive those lands as their own.
And that is just as sure as I am alive."
  The Lord is the God of Israel.

The Lord says, "People of Cush,
  you too will die by my sword."

The Lord will reach out his powerful hand against the
   north.
  He will destroy Assyria.
He'll leave Nineveh totally empty.
  It will be as dry as a desert.
Nineveh was a carefree city.
  It lived in safety.
It said to itself,
  "I am the one!
  No one is greater than I am."

How terrible it will be for Jerusalem!
  Its people crush others.
They refuse to obey the Lord.
  They are "unclean."
They don't obey anyone.
  They don't accept the Lord's warnings.
They don't trust in him.
  They don't ask their God for his help.
Jerusalem's officials are like roaring lions.
  Their rulers are like wolves that hunt in the evening.
  They don't leave anything to eat in the morning.
Their prophets care about nothing.
  They can't be trusted.
Their priests make the temple "unclean."
  They break the law they teach others to obey.
In spite of that, the Lord is good to Jerusalem.
  He never does anything that is wrong.
Every morning he does what is fair.
  Each new day he does the right thing.
But those who do what is wrong
  aren't even ashamed of it.

The Lord says to his people,

"I have destroyed other nations.
  I have wiped out their forts.
I have left their streets deserted.
  No one walks along them.
Their cities are destroyed.
  They are deserted and empty.
Here is what I thought about Jerusalem.
'Surely you will have respect for me.
  Surely you will accept my warning.'
  Then the city you think is safe would not be destroyed.
And I would not have to punish you so much.
  But they still wanted to go on sinning
  in every way they could.
So wait for me to come as judge,"
  announces the Lord.
"Wait for the day I will stand up
  to witness against all sinners.
I have decided to gather the nations.
  I will bring the kingdoms together.
And I will pour out all my burning anger on them.
  The fire of my jealous anger
  will burn the whole world up.

"But then I will purify what all the nations say.
  And they will use their words to worship me.
  They will serve me together.
My scattered people will come to me
  from beyond the rivers of Cush.
They will worship me.
  They will bring me offerings.
Jerusalem, you have done many wrong things to me.
  But at that time you will not be put to shame anymore.
That's because I will remove from this city
  those who think so highly of themselves.

You will never be proud again
on my holy mountain of Zion.
But inside your city I will leave
those who are not proud at all.
Those who are still left alive will trust in the LORD.
They will not do anything wrong.
They will not tell any lies.
They will not say anything to fool other people.
They will eat and lie down in peace.
And no one will make them afraid."

People of Zion, sing!
Israel, shout loudly!
People of Jerusalem, be glad!
Let your hearts be full of joy.
The LORD has stopped punishing you.
He has made your enemies turn away from you.
The LORD is the King of Israel.
He is with you.
You will never again be afraid
that others will harm you.
The time is coming when people will say to Jerusalem,
"Zion, don't be afraid.
Don't give up.
The LORD your God is with you.
He is the Mighty Warrior who saves.
He will take great delight in you.
In his love he will no longer punish you.
Instead, he will sing for joy because of you."

introduction to Nahum

*Everyone knew the Assyrians were very mean and did terrible things
to the nations they invaded. But they were still doing God's work by
judging Israel. Nahum shared with Judah that Assyria was wrong and
would be destroyed for their evil.*

Here is a prophecy the LORD gave Nahum about Nineveh.

The LORD is a jealous God who punishes people.
  He pays them back for the evil things they do.
  He directs his anger against them.
The LORD punishes his enemies.
  He holds his anger back
  until the right time to use it.
The LORD is slow to get angry.
  But he is very powerful.
The LORD will not let guilty people go
  without punishing them.
When he marches out, he stirs up winds and storms.
  Clouds are the dust kicked up by his feet.
He controls the seas. He dries them up.
  He makes all the rivers run dry.

The LORD is good.
  When people are in trouble,
  they can go to him for safety.
He takes good care of those
  who trust in him.
But he will destroy Nineveh
  with a powerful flood.
He will chase his enemies
  into the place of darkness.

The LORD will put an end
  to anything they plan against him.
He won't allow Assyria to win the battle
  over his people a second time.

Look at the mountains of Judah!
  I see a messenger running to bring good news!
  He's telling us that peace has come!

People of Judah, celebrate your feasts.
　　Carry out your promises.
The evil Assyrians won't attack you again.
　　They'll be completely destroyed.

introduction to Habakkuk

Habakkuk spoke at the same time as Nahum. The Babylonian Empire was getting stronger and was about to destroy the Assyrian Empire. Habakkuk was upset that the people of Judah were still not keeping the agreement with God. The evil Assyrians had hurt the people of Judah for a hundred years. Habakkuk thought Judah should have changed how they lived. He was afraid the Babylonians would destroy Judah even though both empires were more evil than Judah. God comforts Habakkuk that he is still in charge of all nations.

❧

This is a prophecy that Habakkuk the prophet received from the Lord.

Lord, how long do I have to call out for help?
　　Why don't you listen to me?
How long must I keep telling you
　　that things are terrible?
　　Why don't you save us?
Why do you make me watch while
　　people treat others so unfairly?
Why do you put up with the wrong things
　　they are doing?
I have to look at death.
　　People are harming others.
　　They are arguing and fighting all the time.
The law can't do what it's supposed to do.
　　Fairness never comes out on top.
Sinful people surround those
　　who do what is right.
　　So people are never treated fairly.

The Lord replies,

"Look at the nations. Watch them.
  Be totally amazed at what you see.
I am going to do something in your days
  that you would never believe.
You would not believe it
  even if someone told you about it.
I am going to send the armies of Babylon to attack you.
  They are very mean. They move quickly.
They terrify others.
  They do not recognize any laws but their own.
  That is how proud they are.
Their horses are faster than leopards.
  They are meaner than wolves at sunset.
They mock kings
  and make fun of rulers.
They sweep past like the wind.
  Then they go on their way.
They are guilty.
  They worship their own strength."

Lord, haven't you existed forever?
  You are my holy God.
  You will never die.
Lord, you have appointed the Babylonians
  to punish your people.
  My Rock, you have chosen them to judge us.
Your eyes are too pure to look at what is evil.
  You can't put up with the wrong things people do.
So why do you put up
  with those who can't be trusted?
The evil Babylonians swallow up
  those who are more godly than themselves.
  So why are you silent?

The LORD replies,

"The message I give you
    waits for the time I have appointed.
It speaks about what is going to happen.
    And all of it will come true.
It might take a while.
    But wait for it.
You can be sure it will come.
    It will happen when I want it to.

"The Babylonians are very proud.
    What they want is not good.

"But the person who is godly
    will live by his faithfulness.

"How terrible it will be for the Babylonians!
    They build cities by spilling the blood of others.
    They establish towns by doing what is wrong.
I am the LORD who rules over all.
    Human effort is no better than wood that feeds a fire.
    So the nations wear themselves out for nothing.
The oceans are full of water.
    In the same way, the earth will be filled
    with the knowledge of my glory.

The LORD is in his holy temple.
    Let the whole earth be silent in front of him.

LORD, I know how famous you are.
    I have great respect for you
    because of your mighty acts.
Do them again for us.
    Make them known in our time.

When you are angry,
please have mercy on us.

I listened and my heart pounded.
My lips trembled at the sound.
My bones seemed to rot.
And my legs shook.
But I will be patient.
I'll wait for the day of trouble to come on Babylon.
It's the nation that is attacking us.
The fig trees might not bud.
The vines might not produce any grapes.
The olive crop might fail.
The fields might not produce any food.
There might not be any sheep in the pens.
There might not be any cattle in the barns.
But I will still be glad
because of what the Lord has done.
God my Savior fills me with joy.

The Lord and King gives me strength.
He makes my feet like the feet of a deer.
He helps me walk on the highest places.

remember what you read

1. What is something you noticed for the first time?

_____

_____

_____

_____

2. What questions did you have?

_____

_____

_____

_____

3. Was there anything that bothered you?

_____

_____

_____

_____

4. What did you learn about loving God?

_____

_____

_____

_____

5. What did you learn about loving others?

_____

_____

_____

_____

introduction to Jeremiah, part 1

Jeremiah spoke in Judah as the Assyrian Empire was falling apart. The people thought they were going to be just fine, since Assyria could no longer attack them. But God warned that this pride would destroy his people. Jeremiah spoke during good King Josiah's reign. He also spoke during the reigns of the last four kings of Judah. These kings were a mess, leading the people to disobey God. They made God's judgment come quickly on Judah and Jerusalem. They were destroyed by the Babylonians.

❧

These are the words Jeremiah received from the LORD. Jeremiah was the son of Hilkiah. A message from the LORD came to Jeremiah. It came in the 13th year that Josiah was king over Judah. After Josiah, his son Jehoiakim was king over Judah. The LORD's message also came to Jeremiah during the whole time Jehoiakim ruled. The LORD continued to speak to Jeremiah while Zedekiah was king over Judah. He did this until the fifth month of the 11th year of Zedekiah's rule. That's when the people of Jerusalem were forced to leave their country. Zedekiah was the son of Josiah. Here is what Jeremiah said.

❧

A message from the LORD came to me. The LORD said,

"Before I formed you in your mother's body I chose you.
    Before you were born I set you apart to serve me.
    I appointed you to be a prophet to the nations."

"You are my LORD and King," I said. "I don't know how to speak. I'm too young."

But the LORD said to me, "Do not say, 'I'm too young.' You must go to everyone I send you to. You must say everything I command you to say. Do not be afraid of the people I send you to. I am with you. I will save you," announces the LORD.

Then the LORD reached out his hand. He touched my mouth and spoke to me. He said, "I have put my words in your mouth. Today I am appointing you to speak to nations and kingdoms. I give you authority to pull them up by the roots and tear them down. I give you authority to destroy them and crush them. I give you authority to build them up and plant them."

A message from the LORD came to me. The LORD asked me, "What do you see, Jeremiah?"

"The branch of an almond tree," I replied.

The LORD said to me, "You have seen correctly. I am watching to see that my word comes true."

Another message from the LORD came to me. The LORD asked me, "What do you see?"

"A pot that has boiling water in it," I answered. "It's leaning toward us from the north."

The LORD said to me, "Something very bad will be poured out on everyone who lives in this land. It will come from the north. I am about to send for all the armies in the northern kingdoms," announces the LORD.

"Their kings will come to Jerusalem.
    They will set up their thrones at the very gates of
        the city.
They will attack all the walls that surround the city.
    They will go to war against all the towns of Judah.
I will judge my people.
    They have done many evil things.
    They have deserted me.
They have burned incense to other gods.
    They have worshiped the gods
    their own hands have made.

"So get ready! Stand up! Tell them everything I command you to. Do not let them terrify you. If you do, I will terrify you in front of them. Today I have made you like a city that has a high wall around it. I have made you like an iron pillar and a bronze wall. Now you can stand up against the whole land. You can stand against the kings and officials of Judah. You can stand against its priests and its people. They will fight against you. But they will not win the battle over you. I am with you. I will save you," announces the Lord.

✣

A message from the Lord came to me. The Lord said, "Go. Announce my message to the people in Jerusalem. I want everyone to hear it. Tell them,

"Here is what the Lord says.

" 'I remember how faithful you were to me when you were
        young.
    You loved me as if you were my bride.
You followed me through the desert.
    Nothing had been planted there.
Your people were holy to me.
    They were the first share of my harvest.
All those who destroyed them were held guilty.
    And trouble came to their enemies,' "
    announces the Lord.

People of Jacob, hear the Lord's message.
    Listen, all you tribes of Israel.

The Lord says,

"What did your people of long ago find wrong with me?
    Why did they wander so far away from me?
They worshiped worthless statues of gods.
    Then they themselves became worthless.
They did not ask, 'Where is the Lord?
    He brought us up out of Egypt.

He led us through a dry and empty land.
   He guided us through deserts and deep valleys.
It was a land of total darkness where there wasn't any rain.
   No one lived or traveled there.'
But I brought you into a land that has rich soil.
   I gave you its fruit and its finest food.
In spite of that, you made my land impure.
   You turned it into something I hate.
The priests did not ask,
   'Where is the LORD?'
Those who taught my law did not know me.
   The leaders refused to obey me.
The prophets prophesied in the name of Baal.
   They worshiped worthless statues of gods.

"So I am bringing charges against you again,"
   announces the LORD.
   "And I will bring charges against your children's
      children.
Has a nation ever changed its gods?
   Actually, they are not even gods at all.
But my people have traded away their glorious God.
   They have traded me for worthless statues of gods.
Sky above, be shocked over this.
   Tremble with horror,"
   announces the LORD.
"My people have sinned twice.
They have deserted me,
   even though I am the spring of water that gives life.
And they have dug their own wells.
   But those wells are broken.
   They can't hold any water.
Are you people of Israel servants?
   You were not born as slaves, were you?
   Then why have you been carried off like stolen goods?
Lions have roared.
   They have growled at you.

They have destroyed your land.
　　Your towns are burned and deserted.
The men of Memphis and Tahpanhes
　　have cracked your skulls.
Haven't you brought this on yourselves?
　　I am the LORD your God, but you deserted me.
　　You left me even while I was leading you.
Why do you go to Egypt
　　to drink water from the Nile River?
Why do you go to Assyria
　　to drink from the Euphrates River?
You will be punished because you have sinned.
　　You will be corrected for turning away from me.
I am the LORD your God.
　　If you desert me, bad things will happen to you.
If you do not respect me, you will suffer bitterly.
　　I want you to understand that,"
　　announces the LORD who rules over all.

"Long ago you broke off the yoke I put on you.
　　You tore off the ropes I tied you up with.
　　You said, 'I won't serve you!'
You were like a good vine when I planted you.
　　You were a healthy plant.
Then how did you turn against me?
　　How did you become a bad, wild vine?
You might wash yourself with soap.
　　You might use plenty of strong soap.
　　But I can still see the stains your guilt covers you with,"
　　announces the LORD and King.
"You say, 'I am "clean."
　　I haven't followed the gods that are named Baal.'
Do not run after other gods
　　until your sandals are worn out and your throat is dry.
But you said, 'It's no use!
　　I love those gods.
　　I must go after them.'

"A thief is dishonored when he is caught.
  And you people of Israel are filled with shame.
Your kings and officials are dishonored.
  So are your priests and your prophets.
You say to a piece of wood, 'You are my father.'
  You say to a stone, 'You are my mother.'
You have turned your backs to me.
  You refuse to look at me.
But when you are in trouble, you say,
  'Come and save us!'
Then where are the gods you made for yourselves?
  Let them come when you are in trouble!
  Let them save you if they can!
Judah, you have as many gods
  as you have towns.

"Why do you bring charges against me?
  All of you have refused to obey me,"
  announces the LORD.
"I punished your people. But it did not do them any
      good.
  They did not pay attention when they were corrected.
You have killed your prophets by swords.
  You have swallowed them up like a hungry lion.

"You who are now living, consider my message. I am saying,

"Have I been like a desert to Israel?
  Have I been like a land of deep darkness?
Why do my people say, 'We are free to wander.
  We won't come to you anymore'?
Does a young woman forget all about her jewelry?
  Does a bride forget her wedding jewels?
But my people have forgotten me
  more days than anyone can count.
The blood of those you have killed is on your clothes.
  You have destroyed poor people who were not guilty.
  You did not catch them in the act of breaking in.

In spite of all this,
   you say, 'I'm not guilty of doing anything wrong.
   The Lord isn't angry with me.'
But I will judge you.
   That's because you say, 'I haven't sinned.'
Why do you keep on
   changing your ways so much?
Assyria did not help you.
   And Egypt will not help you either.
So you will also leave Egypt
   with your hands tied together above your heads.
I have turned my back on those you trust.
   They will not help you.

remember what you read

1. What is something you noticed for the first time?

_____

_____

_____

_____

2. What questions did you have?

_____

_____

_____

_____

3. Was there anything that bothered you?

_____

_____

_____

_____

4. What did you learn about loving God?

_____

_____

_____

_____

5. What did you learn about loving others?

_____

_____

_____

_____

introduction to Jeremiah, part 2

Jeremiah spoke God's message to the people left in the northern land of Israel after it was destroyed by the Assyrians. God promised to restore them, even as he was so angry with Judah for being mean and proud and unfaithful.

∽ᕟᕟ᠊ᢆᠣ

" 'Israel, you have not been faithful,' announces the LORD.
  'Return to me. Then I will do good things for you again.
That's because I am faithful,' announces the LORD.
  'I will not be angry with you forever.
Admit that you are guilty of doing what is wrong.
  You have refused to obey me.
  I am the LORD your God.
You worshiped other gods under every green tree.
  And you have not obeyed me,' "
  announces the LORD.

"You people have not been faithful," announces the LORD. "Return to me. I am your husband. I will choose one of you from each town. I will choose two from each territory. And I will bring you to the city of Zion. Then I will give you shepherds who are dear to my heart. Their knowledge and understanding will help them lead you. In those days there will be many more of you in the land," announces the LORD. "Then people will not talk about the ark of the covenant of the LORD anymore. It will never enter their minds. They will not remember it. The ark will not be missed. And another one will not be made. At that time they will call Jerusalem The Throne of the Lord. All the nations will gather together there. They will go there to honor me. They will no longer do what their stubborn and evil hearts want them to do. In those days the people of Judah will join the people of Israel. Together they will come from a land in the north. They will come to the land I gave to your people of long ago. I wanted them to have it as their very own.

"I myself said,

" 'I would gladly treat you like my children.
    I would give you a pleasant land.
    It is the most beautiful land any nation could have.'
I thought you would call me 'Father.'
    I hoped you would always obey me.
But you people are like a woman who is not faithful to her
        husband.
    Israel, you have not been faithful to me,"
announces the Lord.

A cry is heard on the bare hilltops.
    The people of Israel are weeping and begging for help.
That's because their lives are so twisted.
    They've forgotten the Lord their God.

"You have not been faithful,"
    says the Lord.
"Return to me. I will heal you.
    Then you will not turn away from me anymore."

"Yes," the people say. "We will come to you.
    You are the Lord our God.
The gods we worship on the hills
    and mountains are useless.
You are the Lord our God.
    You are the only one who can save us.
From our earliest years shameful gods have harmed us.
    They have eaten up everything our people of long ago
        worked for.

They have eaten up our flocks and herds.
    They've destroyed our sons and daughters.
Let us lie down in our shame.
    Let our dishonor cover us.
You are the LORD our God. But we have sinned against you.
    We and our people of long ago have sinned.
We haven't obeyed you
    from our earliest years until now."

Here is what the LORD is telling the people of Judah and Jerusalem. He says,

"Your hearts are as hard as a field
    that has not been plowed.
So change your ways and produce good crops.
    Do not plant seeds among thorns.
People of Judah and you who live in Jerusalem, obey me.
    Do not let your hearts be stubborn.
If you do, my anger will blaze out against you.
    It will burn like fire because of the evil things you have
        done.
    No one will be able to put it out.

❦

The LORD says, "My people are foolish.
    They do not know me.
They are children who do not have any sense.
    They have no understanding at all.
They are skilled in doing what is evil.
    They do not know how to do what is good."

I looked at the earth.
    It didn't have any shape. And it was empty.
I looked at the sky.
    Its light was gone.
I looked at the mountains.
    They were shaking.
    All the hills were swaying.

I looked. And there weren't any people.
  Every bird in the sky had flown away.
I looked. And the fruitful land had become a desert.
  All its towns were destroyed.
  The Lord had done all this because of his great anger.

ᏬᏬᎧ

The Lord says, "Go up and down the streets of Jerusalem.
  Look around.
  Think about what you see.
Search through the market.
  See if you can find one honest person who tries to be
    truthful.
  If you can, I will forgive this city.
They make their promises in my name.
  They say, 'You can be sure that the Lord is alive.'
  But their promises can't be trusted."

Lord, don't your eyes look for truth?
  You struck down your people.
  But they didn't feel any pain.
You crushed them.
  But they refused to be corrected.
They made their faces harder than stone.
  They refused to turn away from their sins.
I thought, "The people of
  Jerusalem are foolish.
They don't know how the Lord wants them to live.
  They don't know what their God requires of them.
So I will go to the leaders.
  I'll speak to them.
They should know how the Lord wants them to live.
  They must know what their God requires of them."
But all of them had broken off the yoke the Lord had put on
    them.
  They had torn off the ropes he had tied them up with.

So a lion from the forest will attack them.
  A wolf from the desert will destroy them.
A leopard will hide and wait near their towns.
  It will tear to pieces anyone who dares to go out.
Again and again they have refused to obey the Lord.
  They have turned away from him many times.

"Armies of Babylon, go through their vineyards and destroy
    them.
  But do not destroy them completely.
Strip off their branches.
  These people do not belong to me.
The people of Israel and the people of Judah
  have not been faithful to me at all,"
  announces the Lord.

They have told lies about the Lord.
  They said, "He won't do anything!
No harm will come to us.
  We will never see war or be hungry.
The prophets are nothing but wind.
  Their message doesn't come from the Lord.
  So let what they say will happen be done to them."

The Lord God rules over all. He says to me,

"The people have spoken these words.
  So my words will be like fire in your mouth.
I will make the people like wood.
  And the fire will burn them up."

"In spite of that, even in those days I will not destroy you completely," announces the Lord. 'Jeremiah,' the people will ask, 'Why
has the Lord our God done all this to us?' Then you will tell them,
'You have deserted the Lord. You have served other gods in your
own land. So now you will serve another nation in a land that is
not your own.'

"Here is what I want you to announce
  to the people of Jacob.

Tell it in Judah.
  Tell them I say,
'Listen to this, you foolish people,
  who do not have any sense.
You have eyes, but you do not see.
  You have ears, but you do not hear.
Shouldn't you have respect for me?'
  announces the LORD.
  'Shouldn't you tremble with fear in front of me?

"Something horrible and shocking
  has happened in the land.
The prophets prophesy lies.
  The priests rule by their own authority.
And my people love it this way.
  But what will you do in the end?"

ͽͽͽ

The LORD tells the people of Judah,

"Stand where the roads cross, and look around.
  Ask where the old paths are.
Ask for the good path, and walk on it.
  Then your hearts will find rest in me.
  But you said, 'We won't walk on it.'
I appointed prophets to warn you. I said,
  'Listen to the sound of the trumpets!'
  But you said, 'We won't listen.'
So pay attention, you nations.
  You are witnesses for me.
  Watch what will happen to my people.
Earth, pay attention.
  I am going to bring trouble on them.
  I will punish them because of the evil things they have
    done.
They have not listened to my words.
  They have said no to my law.

What do I care about incense from the land of Sheba?
  Why should I bother with sweet-smelling cane from a land
    far away?
I do not accept your burnt offerings.
  Your sacrifices do not please me."

So the LORD says,

"I will bring an army against the people of Judah.
  Parents and children alike will trip and fall.
  Neighbors and friends will die."

The LORD says to Jerusalem,

"Look! An army is coming
  from the land of the north.
I am stirring up a great nation.
  Its army is coming from a land that is very far away.
Its soldiers are armed with bows and spears.
  They are mean. They do not show any mercy at all.
They come riding in on their horses.
  They sound like the roaring ocean.
They are lined up for battle.
  They are marching out
    to attack you, city of Zion."

We have heard reports about them.
  And our hands can't help us.
We are suffering greatly.
  It's like the pain of a woman having a baby.
Don't go out to the fields.
  Don't walk on the roads.
Our enemies have swords.
  And there is terror on every side.
My people, put on the clothes of sadness.
  Roll among the ashes.
Mourn with bitter weeping
  just as you would mourn for an only son.
The one who is going to destroy us
  will come suddenly.

The LORD says to me, "I have made you like one who tests
   metals.
   My people are the ore.
I want you to watch them
   and test the way they live.
All of them are used to disobeying me.
   They go around telling lies about others.
They are like bronze mixed with iron.
   All of them do very sinful things.
The fire is made very hot
   so the lead will burn away.
But it is impossible to make these people pure.
   Those who are evil are not removed.
They are like silver that is thrown away.
   That is because I have not accepted them."

remember what you read

1. What is something you noticed for the first time?

_____

_____

_____

_____

2. What questions did you have?

_____

_____

_____

_____

3. Was there anything that bothered you?

_____

_____

_____

_____

4. What did you learn about loving God?

_____

_____

_____

_____

5. What did you learn about loving others?

_____

_____

_____

_____

introduction to Jeremiah, part 3

God often asked Jeremiah to do something with his body or an object to help the people understand what God was going to do. In today's reading, Jeremiah continues to speak God's words to the people of Jerusalem and Judah.

∽∾∿∽

A message from the LORD came to Jeremiah. The LORD said, "Stand at the gate of my house. Announce my message to the people there. Say,

"'Listen to the LORD's message, all you people of Judah. You always come through these gates to worship the LORD. The God of Israel is speaking to you. He is the LORD who rules over all. He says, "Change the way you live and act. Then I will let you live in this place. Do not trust in lies. Do not say, 'This is the temple of the LORD! This is the temple of the LORD! This is the temple of the LORD!' You must really change the way you live and act. Treat one another fairly. Do not treat outsiders or widows badly in this place. Do not take advantage of children whose fathers have died. Do not kill those who are not guilty of doing anything wrong. Do not worship other gods. That will only bring harm to you. If you obey me, I will let you live in this place. It is the land I gave your people of long ago. It was promised to them for ever and ever. But look! You are trusting in worthless lies.

"'"You continue to steal and commit murder. You commit adultery. You tell lies in court. You burn incense to Baal. You worship other gods you didn't know before. Then you come and stand in front of me. You keep coming to this house where I have put my Name. You say, 'We are safe.' You think you are safe when you do so many things I hate. My Name is in this house. But you have made it a den for robbers! I have been watching you!" announces the Lord.

" ' "Go now to the town of Shiloh. Go to the place where I first made a home for my Name. See what I did to it because of the evil things my people Israel were doing. I spoke to you again and again," announces the Lord. "I warned you while you were doing all these things. But you did not listen. I called out to you. But you did not answer. So what I did to Shiloh I will now do to the house where my Name is. It is the temple you trust in. It is the place I gave to you and your people of long ago. But I will throw you out of my land. That is exactly what I did to the people of Ephraim. And they are your relatives." '

So the Lord and King says, "I will pour out my burning anger on this place. It will strike people and animals alike. It will destroy the trees in the fields and the crops in your land. It will burn, and no one will be able to put it out."

"Jeremiah, when you tell them all this, they will not listen to you. When you call out to them, they will not answer. So say to them, 'You are a nation that has not obeyed the Lord your God. You did not pay attention when you were corrected. Truth has died out. You do not tell the truth anymore.' "

The Lord says to the people of Jerusalem, "Cut off your hair. Throw it away. Sing a song of sadness on the bare hilltops. I am very angry with you. I have turned my back on you. I have deserted you."

"Jeremiah, tell them, 'The Lord says,

" ' "How can you people say, 'We are wise.
    We have the law of the Lord'?
Actually, the teachers of the law have told lies about it.
    Their pens have not written what is true.

Those who think they are wise will be put to shame.
    They will become terrified. They will be trapped.
They have not accepted my message.
    So what kind of wisdom do they have?
I will give their wives to other men.
    I will give their fields to new owners.
Everyone wants to get richer and richer.
    Everyone is greedy, from the least important to the most
        important.
Prophets and priests alike
    try to fool everyone they can.
They bandage the wounds of my people
    as if they were not very deep.
'Peace, peace,' they say.
    But there isn't any peace.
Are they ashamed of their hateful actions?
    No. They do not feel any shame at all.
    They do not even know how to blush.
So they will fall like others who have already fallen.
    They will be brought down when I punish them,"
    says the LORD.

LORD, my heart is weak inside me.
    You comfort me when I'm sad.
Listen to the cries of my people
    from a land far away.
They cry out, "Isn't the LORD in Zion?
    Isn't its King there anymore?"

The LORD says, "Why have they made me so angry
    by worshiping their wooden gods?
Why have they made me angry
    with their worthless statues
    of gods from other lands?"

The people say, "The harvest is over.
    The summer has ended.
    And we still haven't been saved."

My people are crushed, so I am crushed.
 I mourn, and I am filled with horror.
Isn't there any healing lotion in Gilead?
 Isn't there a doctor there?
Then why doesn't someone heal
 the wounds of my people?

I wish my head were a spring of water!
 I wish my eyes were a fountain of tears!
I would weep day and night
 for my people who have been killed.

"They get ready to use
 their tongues like bows,"
 announces the Lord.
"Their mouths shoot out lies like arrows.
 They tell lies to gain power in the land.
They go from one sin to another.
 They do not pay any attention to me.
Be on guard against your friends.
 Do not trust the members of your own family.
Every one of them cheats.
 Every friend tells lies.
One friend cheats another.
 No one tells the truth.
They have taught their tongues how to lie.
 They wear themselves out sinning.
Jeremiah, you live among people who tell lies.
 When they lie, they refuse to pay any attention
  to me,"
 announces the Lord.

So the Lord who rules over all says,

"I will put them through the fire to test them.
 What else can I do?
 My people are so sinful!
Their tongues are like deadly arrows.
 They tell lies.

With their mouths all of them speak kindly to their
neighbors.
But in their hearts they set traps for them.
Shouldn't I punish them for this?"
announces the LORD.
"Shouldn't I pay back the nation
that does these things?"

The LORD says,

"Do not let wise people brag about how wise they are.
Do not let strong people boast about how strong they are.
Do not let rich people brag about how rich they are.
But here is what the one who brags should boast about.
They should brag that they have the understanding to
know me.
I want them to know that I am the LORD.
No matter what I do on earth, I am always kind, fair and
right.
And I take delight in this,"
announces the LORD.

"The days are coming when I will judge people," announces the
LORD. "I will punish all those who are circumcised only in their
bodies. That includes the people of Egypt, Judah, Edom, Ammon
and Moab. It also includes all those who live in the desert in places
far away. None of the people in these nations is really circumcised.
And not even the people of Israel are circumcised in their hearts."

ᘉᘉᘉ

LORD, I know that a person doesn't control their own life.
They don't direct their own steps.
Correct me, LORD, but please be fair.
Don't correct me when you are angry.
If you do, nothing will be left of me.
Pour out your great anger on the nations.
They don't pay any attention to you.
They refuse to worship you.

They have destroyed the people of Jacob.
They've wiped them out completely.
They've also destroyed the land they lived in.

⟨∂∂∂⟩

The Lord said to me, "Here is what I want you to announce in the towns of Judah. Say it also in the streets of Jerusalem. Tell the people, 'Listen to the terms of my covenant. Obey them. Long ago I brought your people up from Egypt. From that time until today, I warned them again and again. I said, "Obey me." But they did not listen. They did not pay any attention to me. Instead, they did what their stubborn and evil hearts wanted them to do. So I brought down on them all the curses of the covenant. I commanded them to obey it. But they refused.' "

"Jeremiah, do not pray for these people. Do not make any appeal or request for them. They will call out to me when they are in trouble. But I will not listen to them.

"I love the people of Judah.
   But they are working out their evil plans along with many
      others.
   So what are they doing in my temple?
Can meat that is offered to me keep me from punishing you?
   When you do evil things, you get a lot of pleasure from
      them."

People of Judah, the Lord once called you a healthy olive
      tree.
   He thought its fruit was beautiful.
But now he will come with the roar of a mighty storm.
   He will set the tree on fire.
   And its branches will be broken.

The Lord who rules over all planted you. But now he has ordered your enemies to destroy you. The people of Israel and Judah have both done what is evil. They have made the Lord very angry by burning incense to Baal.

Lord, when I bring a matter to you,
　you always do what is right.
But now I would like to speak with you
　about whether you are being fair.
Why are sinful people successful?
　Why do those who can't be trusted have an easy life?
You have planted them.
　Their roots are deep in the ground.
　They grow and produce fruit.
They honor you by what they say.
　But their hearts are far away from you.
Lord, you know me and see me.
　You test my thoughts about you.
Drag those people off like sheep to be killed!
　Set them apart for the day of their death!
How long will the land be thirsty for water?
　How long will the grass in every field be dry?
The people who live in the land are evil.
　So the animals and birds have died.
And that's not all. The people are saying,
　"The Lord won't see what happens to us."

Here is what the Lord says. "All my evil neighbors have taken over the land I gave my people Israel. So I will pull them up by their roots from the lands they live in. And I will pull up the roots of the people of Judah from among them. But after I pull up those nations, I will give my tender love to them again. I will bring all of them back to their own lands. I will take all of them back to their own countries. Suppose those nations learn to follow the practices of my people. And they make their promises in my name. When they promise, they say, 'You can be sure that the Lord is alive.' They do this just as they once taught my people to make promises in Baal's name. Then I will give them a place among my people. But what if one of those nations does not listen? Then you can be sure of this. I will pull it up by the roots and destroy it," announces the Lord.

remember what you read

1. What is something you noticed for the first time?

_____

_____

_____

_____

2. What questions did you have?

_____

_____

_____

_____

3. Was there anything that bothered you?

_____

_____

_____

_____

4. What did you learn about loving God?

_____

_____

_____

_____

5. What did you learn about loving others?

_____

_____

_____

_____

JEREMIAH, PART 4

introduction to Jeremiah, part 4

Jeremiah continues doing things with objects and speaking God's words to show the people the judgment about to come upon them.

❦

The LORD said to me, "Go and buy a linen belt. Put it around your waist. But do not let it get wet." So I bought a belt, just as the LORD had told me to do. And I put it around my waist.

Then another message from the LORD came to me. The LORD said, "Take off the belt you bought and are wearing around your waist. Go to Perath. Hide the belt there in a crack in the rocks." So I went and hid it at Perath. I did just as the LORD had told me to do.

Many days later the LORD said to me, "Go to Perath. Get the belt I told you to hide there." So I went to Perath. I dug up the belt. I took it from the place where I had hidden it. But it had rotted. It was completely useless.

Then another message from the LORD came to me. The LORD said, "In the same way, I will destroy Judah's pride. And I will destroy the great pride of Jerusalem. These people are evil. They refuse to listen to what I say. They do what their stubborn hearts want them to do. They chase after other gods. They serve them and worship them. So they will be like this belt. They will be completely useless. A belt is tied around a person's waist. In the same way, I tied all the people of Israel to me. I also tied all the people of Judah to me like a belt. I wanted them to be my people. They should have brought me fame and praise and honor. But they have not listened to me," announces the LORD.

People of Judah, listen to me.
　Pay attention and don't be proud.
　The LORD has spoken.
Give glory to the LORD your God.
　Honor him before he sends
　darkness to cover the land.
Do this before you trip and fall
　on the darkened hills.
You hope that light will come.
　But he will turn it into thick darkness.
　He will change it to deep shadows.
If you don't listen,
　I will weep in secret.
　Because you are so proud,
I will weep bitterly.
　Tears will flow from my eyes.
　The LORD's flock will be taken away as prisoners.

Speak to the king and his mother. Tell them,
　"Come down from your thrones.
Your glorious crowns
　are about to fall from your heads."
The gates of the cities in the Negev Desert will be shut tight.
　There won't be anyone to open them.
Everyone in Judah will be carried away as prisoners.
　You will be completely taken away.

A message from the LORD came to Jeremiah. He told Jeremiah there wouldn't be any rain in the land. The LORD said,

"Judah is filled with sadness.
　Its cities are wasting away.
The people weep for the land.
　Crying is heard in Jerusalem.

The nobles send their servants to get water.
　They go to the wells.
　But they do not find any water.
They return with empty jars.
　They are terrified. They do not have any hope.
　They cover their heads.
The ground is dry and cracked.
　There isn't any rain in the land.
The farmers are terrified.
　They cover their heads.
Even the female deer in the fields
　desert their newborn fawns.
　There isn't any grass to eat.
Wild donkeys stand on the bare hilltops.
　They long for water as wild dogs do.
Their eyesight fails
　because they do not have any food to eat."

Lord, our sins are a witness against us.
　But do something for the honor of your name.
We have often turned away from you.
　We've sinned against you.
You are Israel's only hope.
　You save us when we're in trouble.
Why are you like a stranger to us?
　Why are you like a traveler who stays for only one
　　night?
Why are you like a man taken by surprise?
　Why are you like a soldier who can't save anyone?
Lord, you are among us.
　And we are your people.
　Please don't desert us!
"Jeremiah, give them this message. Tell them,

Lord, have you completely turned your back on Judah?
　Do you hate the city of Zion?
Why have you made us suffer?
　We can't be healed.

We hoped peace would come.
  But nothing good has happened to us.
We hoped we would finally be healed.
  But all we got was terror.
LORD, we admit we've done evil things.
  We also admit that our people of long ago were guilty.
  It's true that we've sinned against you.
For the honor of your name, don't turn your back on us.
  Don't bring shame on your glorious throne in the
    temple.
Remember the covenant you made with us.
  Please don't break it.
Do any of the worthless gods of the nations bring rain?
  Do the skies send down showers all by themselves?
No. LORD our God, you send the rain.
  So we put our hope in you.
  You are the one who does all these things.

Then the LORD said to me, "Suppose Moses and Samuel were standing in front of me. Even then my heart would not feel sorry for these people. Send them away from me! Let them go! Suppose these people ask you, 'Where should we go?' Then tell them, 'The LORD says,

" ' "Those I have appointed to die will die.
Those I have appointed to be killed by swords
  will be killed by swords.
Those I have appointed to die of hunger
  will die of hunger.
Those I have appointed to be taken away as prisoners
  will be taken away." ' "

My mother, I wish I had never been born!
  The whole land opposes me.
  They fight against me.
I haven't made loans to anyone.
  And I haven't borrowed anything.
  But everyone curses me anyway.

The LORD said,

"Jeremiah, I will keep you safe for a good purpose.
  I will make your enemies ask you to pray for them.
They will make their appeal to you
  when they are in great trouble.

"People of Judah, the armies of Babylon
  will come from the north.
They are as strong as iron and bronze.
  Can anyone break their power?
I will give away your wealth and your treasures.
  Your enemies will carry off everything.
  And they will not pay anything for it.
That will happen because you have sinned so much.
  You have done it throughout your country.
I will make you slaves to your enemies.
  You will serve them in a land
  you have not known about before.
My anger will start a fire
  that will burn you up."

LORD, you understand how much I'm suffering.
  Show concern for me. Take care of me.
  Pay back those who are trying to harm me.
You are patient. Don't take my life away from me.
  Think about how much shame I suffer because of you.
When I received your words, I ate them.
  They filled me with joy.
  My heart took delight in them.
LORD God who rules over all,
  I belong to you.
I never sat around with those who go to wild parties.
  I never had a good time with them.
I sat alone because you had put your powerful hand on me.
  Your anger against sin was burning inside me.
Why does my pain never end?
  Why is my wound so deep?
  Why can't I ever get well?

To me you are like a stream that runs dry.
　You are like a spring that doesn't have any water.

So the LORD says to Jeremiah,

"If you turn away from your sins, I will heal you.
　And then you will be able to serve me.
Speak words that are worthy, not worthless.
　Then you will be speaking for me.
Let these people turn to you.
　But you must not turn to them.
I will make you like a wall to them.
　I will make you like a strong bronze wall.
The people will fight against you.
　But they will not overcome you.
I am with you.
　I will save you,"
announces the LORD.
"I will save you from the hands of evil people.
　I will set you free from those who treat you badly."

∞∞∞

The LORD says,

"Those who trust in human beings are under my curse.
　They depend on human strength.
　Their hearts turn away from me.
They will be like a bush in a dry and empty land.
　They will not enjoy success when it comes.
They will live in dry places in the desert.
　It is a land of salt where no one else lives.

"But I will bless anyone who trusts in me.
　I will do good things for the person who depends on me.
They will be like a tree planted near water.
　It sends out its roots beside a stream.
It is not afraid when heat comes.
　Its leaves are always green.

It does not worry when there is no rain.
  It always bears fruit."

A human heart is more dishonest than anything else.
  It can't be healed.
  Who can understand it?

The Lord says, "I look deep down inside human hearts.
  I see what is in people's minds.
I reward each person in keeping with their conduct.
  I bless them based on what they have done."

Some people get rich by doing sinful things.
  They are like a partridge that hatches eggs it didn't lay.
When their lives are half over, their riches will desert them.
  In the end they will prove how foolish they have been.

remember what you read

1. What is something you noticed for the first time?

_____

_____

_____

_____

2. What questions did you have?

_____

_____

_____

_____

3. Was there anything that bothered you?

_____

_____

_____

_____

4. What did you learn about loving God?

_____

_____

_____

_____

5. What did you learn about loving others?

_____

_____

_____

_____

JEREMIAH, PART 5

introduction to Jeremiah, part 5

In today's reading, we hear how hard it was for Jeremiah to speak God's message. The things he said were so unpopular even his friends were looking for ways to get rid of him. God told Jeremiah to speak to different people about how they lived. He spoke to kings and prophets who were not actually hearing from God but telling lies. But God also encouraged Jeremiah at the end of our reading by saying that his people have never listened to prophets who spoke the truth. Notice God's big promise of a good King who would come. Who do you think that is?

A message from the LORD came to me. He said, "Jeremiah, go down to the potter's house. I will give you my message there." So I went down to the potter's house. I saw him working at his wheel. His hands were shaping a pot out of clay. But he saw that something was wrong with it. So he formed it into another pot. He shaped it in the way that seemed best to him.

Then the LORD's message came to me. "People of Israel, I can do with you just as this potter does," announces the LORD. "The clay is in the potter's hand. And you are in my hand, people of Israel. Suppose I announce that something will happen to a nation or kingdom. Suppose I announce that it will be pulled up by the roots. And I announce that it will be torn down and destroyed. But suppose the nation I warned turns away from its sins. Then I will not do what I said I would. I will not bring trouble on it as I had planned. But suppose I announce that a nation or kingdom is going to be built up and planted. And then it does what is evil in my eyes. It does not obey me. Then I will think again about the good things I had wanted to do for it.

"So speak to the people of Judah and Jerusalem. Tell them, 'The LORD says, "Look! I am making plans against you. I am going to bring trouble on you. So each one of you must turn from your evil ways. Change the way you live and act."' But they will reply, 'It's no use. We will continue to do what we've already planned. All of us will do what our stubborn and evil hearts want us to do.'"

They said, "Come on. Let's make plans against Jeremiah. We'll still have priests to teach us the law. We'll always have wise people to give us advice. We'll have prophets to bring us messages from the LORD. So come on. Let's speak out against Jeremiah. We shouldn't pay any attention to what he says."

LORD, please listen to me!
    Hear what my enemies are saying about me!
Should the good things I've done be paid back with evil?
    But my enemies have dug a pit for me.
Remember that I stood in front of you
    and spoke up for them.
    I tried to turn your anger away from them.
Bring their enemies against them without warning.
    Let cries be heard from their houses.
They have dug a pit to capture me.
    They have hidden traps for my feet.
But LORD, you know
    all about their plans to kill me.
Don't forgive their crimes.
    Don't erase their sins from your sight.
Destroy my enemies.
    Punish them when the time to show your anger comes.

Every time I speak, I cry out.
    All you ever tell me to talk about
    is fighting and trouble.

Your message has brought me nothing but dishonor.
  It has made me suffer shame all day long.
Sometimes I think, "I won't talk about his message
    anymore.
  I'll never speak in his name again."
But then your message burns in my heart.
  It's like a fire deep inside my bones.
I'm tired of holding it in.
  In fact, I can't.
I hear many people whispering,
  "There is terror on every side!
  Bring charges against Jeremiah! Let's bring charges
    against him!"
All my friends
  are waiting for me to slip.
They are saying, "Perhaps he will be tricked
  into making a mistake.
Then we'll win out over him.
  We'll get even with him."

But you are with me like a mighty warrior.
  So those who are trying to harm me will trip and fall.
  They won't win out over me.
They will fail. They'll be totally put to shame.
  Their dishonor will never be forgotten.

Lord, you rule over all.
  You test those who do what is right.
  You see what is in people's hearts and minds.
So pay them back for what they've done.
  I've committed my cause to you.

Sing to the Lord, you people!
  Give praise to him!
He saves the lives of people in need.
  He saves them from the power of sinful people.

A message from the Lord came to Jeremiah. It came when King Zedekiah sent Pashhur to Jeremiah. Pashhur was the son of Malkijah. Zedekiah sent Zephaniah the priest along with him. Zephaniah was the son of Maaseiah. They said to Jeremiah, "Ask the Lord to help us. Nebuchadnezzar king of Babylon is attacking us. In the past the Lord did wonderful things for us. Maybe he'll do them again. Then Nebuchadnezzar will pull his armies back from us."

But Jeremiah answered them, "Tell Zedekiah and his people, 'The Lord is the God of Israel. He says, "The king of Babylon and his armies are all around this city. They are getting ready to attack you. You have weapons of war in your hands to fight against them. But I am about to turn your weapons against you. And I will bring your enemies inside this city. I myself will fight against you. I will reach out my powerful hand and mighty arm. I will come against you with all my great anger. I will strike down those who live in this city. I will kill people and animals alike. They will die of a terrible plague. After that, I will hand you over to your enemies. They want to kill you," announces the Lord. "I will hand over Zedekiah, the king of Judah, and his officials. I will also hand over the people in this city who live through the plague, war and hunger. All of them will be handed over to Nebuchadnezzar, the king of Babylon. He will kill them with swords. He will show them no mercy. He will not feel sorry for them. In fact, he will not have any concern for them at all." '

"Tell the people, 'The Lord says, "I am offering you a choice. You can choose the way that leads to life. Or you can choose the way that leads to death. Those who stay in this city will die of war, hunger or plague. But suppose some go out and give themselves up to the Babylonians attacking you. They will live. They will escape with their lives. I have decided to do this city harm and not good," announces the Lord. "It will be handed over to the king of Babylon. And he will destroy it with fire." '

"King Jehoiachin, you are the son of Jehoiakim," announces the Lord. "Suppose you were a ring on my right hand. And suppose the ring even had my royal mark on it. Then I would still pull you off my finger. And that is just as sure as I am alive. I will hand you over to those who want to kill you. I will hand you over to people you are afraid of. I will give you to Nebuchadnezzar, the king of Babylon. I will hand you over to his armies. I will throw you out into another country. I will throw your mother out. Neither of you was born in that country. But both of you will die there. You will never come back to the land you long to return to."

This man Jehoiachin is like a broken pot.
 Everyone hates him. No one wants him.
Why will he and his children be thrown out of this land?
 Why will they be sent to a land
 they don't know about?
Land, land, land,
 listen to the LORD's message!
The LORD says,
"Let the record say that this man did not have any children.
 Let it report that he did not have any success in life.
None of his children will have success either.
 None of them will sit on David's throne.
 None of them will ever rule over Judah.

⁓⁓⁓

"How terrible it will be for the shepherds who lead my people astray!" announces the LORD. "They are destroying and scattering the sheep that belong to my flock." So the LORD, the God of Israel, speaks to the shepherds who take care of my people. He tells them, "You have scattered my sheep. You have driven them away. You have not taken good care of them. So I will punish you for the evil things you have done," announces the LORD. "I myself will gather together those who are left alive in my flock. I will gather them out of all the countries where I have driven them. And I will bring them back to their own land. There my sheep will have many lambs. There will be many more of them. I will place shepherds over them who will take good care of them. My sheep will not be afraid or terrified anymore. And none of them will be missing," announces the LORD.

"A new day is coming," announces the LORD.
"At that time I will raise up for David's royal line
a godly Branch.
He will be a King who will rule wisely.
He will do what is fair and right in the land.
In his days Judah will be saved.
Israel will live in safety.
And the Branch will be called
The LORD Who Makes Us Right With Himself.

Other days are also coming," announces the LORD. "At that time people will no longer say, 'The LORD brought the Israelites up out of Egypt. And that's just as sure as he is alive.' Instead, they will say, 'The LORD brought the Israelites up out of the land of the north. He gathered them out of all the countries where he had forced them to go. And that's just as sure as he is alive.' Then they will live in their own land."

remember what you read

1. What is something you noticed for the first time?

_____

_____

_____

_____

2. What questions did you have?

_____

_____

_____

_____

3. Was there anything that bothered you?

_____

_____

_____

_____

4. What did you learn about loving God?

_____

_____

_____

_____

5. What did you learn about loving others?

_____

_____

_____

_____

introduction to Jeremiah, part 6

Jeremiah continues to risk his life by pleading with the people and leaders to listen to God's message and obey him. If they obeyed, they might not be killed by Babylon. But if they stayed proud against God, very bad things would happen to them.

❦

"I have heard what the prophets are saying. They prophesy lies in my name. They say, 'I had a dream! The LORD has given me a dream!' How long will that continue in the hearts of these prophets who tell lies? They try to get others to believe their own mistaken ideas. They tell one another their dreams. They think that will make my people forget my name. In the same way, their people of long ago forgot my name when they worshiped Baal. Let the prophet who has a dream describe the dream. But let the one who has my message speak it faithfully. Your prophets have given you straw to eat instead of grain," announces the LORD. "My message is like fire," announces the LORD. "It is like a hammer that breaks a rock in pieces.

"So I am against these prophets," announces the LORD. "I am against those who steal messages from one another. They claim that the messages come from me. Yes," announces the LORD. "I am against the prophets who speak their own words. But they still say, 'Here is what the LORD says.' I am against prophets who talk about dreams that did not come from me," announces the LORD. "They tell foolish lies. Their lies lead my people astray. But I did not send these prophets. I did not appoint them. They do not help my people in the least," announces the LORD.

❧

"The LORD has sent all his servants the prophets to you. They've come to you again and again. But you haven't listened. You haven't paid any attention to them. They said, 'Each of you must turn from your evil ways and practices. Then you can stay in the land forever. It's the land the LORD gave you and your people of long ago. Don't follow other gods. Don't serve them or worship them. Don't make the LORD angry with the gods your own hands have made. Then he won't harm you.'

" 'But you did not listen to me,' announces the LORD. 'You have made me very angry with the gods your hands have made. And you have brought harm on yourselves.'

❧

The LORD who rules over all says,

"Look! Horrible trouble is spreading
    from one nation to another.
A mighty storm is rising.
    It is coming from a place
    that is very far away."

Weep and cry, you shepherds.
    Roll in the dust, you leaders of the flock.
Your time to be killed has come.
    You will fall like the best of the rams.
The shepherds won't have any place to run to.
    The leaders of the flock won't be able to escape.
Listen to the cries of the shepherds.
    Hear the weeping of the leaders of the flock.
    The LORD is destroying their grasslands.
Their peaceful meadows will be completely destroyed
    because of the LORD's great anger.

Like a lion he will leave his den.
    The land of those leaders will become a desert.
That's because the sword of the LORD brings great
        harm.
    His anger will burn against them.

∽ᎧᎧ∾

A message from the LORD came to Jeremiah. It was shortly after Jehoiakim became king of Judah. He was the son of Josiah. The LORD said to Jeremiah, "Stand in the courtyard of my house. Speak to the people of the towns in Judah. Speak to all those who come to worship in my house. Tell them everything I command you. Do not leave out a single word. Perhaps they will listen. Maybe they will turn from their evil ways. Then I will not do what I said I would. I will not bring trouble on them. I had planned to punish them because of the evil things they had done. Tell them, 'The LORD says, "Listen to me. Obey my law that I gave you. And listen to the words my servants the prophets are speaking. I have sent them to you again and again. But you have not listened to them. So I will make this house like Shiloh. All the nations on earth will use the name of this city in a curse." ' "

Jeremiah spoke these words in the LORD's house. The priests, the prophets and all the people heard him. Jeremiah finished telling all the people everything the LORD had commanded him to say. But as soon as he did, the priests, the prophets and all the people grabbed him. They said, "You must die! Why do you prophesy these things in the LORD's name? Why do you say that this house will become like Shiloh? Why do you say that this city will be empty and deserted?" And all the people crowded around Jeremiah in the LORD's house.

Then the officials and all the people spoke to the priests and prophets. They said, "This man shouldn't be sentenced to death! He has spoken to us in the name of the LORD our God."

Some of the elders of the land stepped forward. They spoke to the whole community gathered there. They said, "Micah from Moresheth prophesied. It was during the time Hezekiah was king over Judah. Micah spoke to all the people of Judah. He told them, 'The Lord who rules over all says,

"'"Zion will be plowed up like a field.
   Jerusalem will be turned into a pile of trash.
   The temple hill will be covered with bushes and weeds."'

Did King Hezekiah or anyone else in Judah put Micah to death? Hezekiah had respect for the Lord and tried to please him. And the Lord didn't judge Jerusalem as he said he would. He didn't bring on it the trouble he said he would bring. But we are about to bring horrible trouble on ourselves!"

⁓ᗧᗧᕲ

Jeremiah the prophet sent a letter from Jerusalem to Babylon. It was for the Jewish elders still alive there. It was also for the priests and prophets in Babylon. And it was for all the other people Nebuchadnezzar had taken from Jerusalem to Babylon.

The Lord who rules over all is the God of Israel. He speaks to all those he forced to go from Jerusalem to Babylon. He says, "Build houses and make your homes there. Plant gardens and eat what they produce. Get married. Have sons and daughters. Find wives for your sons. Give your daughters to be married. Then they too can have sons and daughters. Let there be many more of you and not fewer. Also work for the success of the city I have sent you to. Pray to the Lord for that city. If it succeeds, you too will enjoy success." The Lord who rules over all is the God of Israel. He says, "Do not let the prophets trick you. Do not be fooled by those who claim to have secret knowledge. Do not listen to people who try to explain their dreams to you. All of them are prophesying lies to you in my name. I have not sent them," announces the Lord.

The Lord says, "You will be forced to live in Babylon for 70 years. After they are over, I will come to you. My good promise to you will come true. I will bring you back home. I know the plans I have for you," announces the Lord. "I want you to enjoy success. I do not plan to harm you. I will give you hope for the years to come. Then you will call out to me. You will come and pray to me. And I will listen to you. When you look for me with all your heart, you will find me. I will be found by you," announces the LORD. "And I will bring you back from where you were taken as prisoners. I will gather you from all the nations. I will gather you from the places where I have forced you to go," announces the LORD. "I will bring you back to the place I sent you away from."

⟨⟨⟨⟨⟨

A message from the LORD came to Jeremiah. The LORD said, "I am the LORD. I am the God of Israel. I say, 'Write in a book all the words I have spoken to you. A new day is coming,'" announces the LORD. "'At that time I will bring my people Israel and Judah back from where they have been taken as prisoners. I will bring them back to this land. I gave it to their people of long ago to have as their own,'" says the LORD.

The LORD says,

"I will bless Jacob's people with great success again.
　　I will show tender love to Israel.
Jerusalem will be rebuilt where it was destroyed.
　　The palace will stand in its proper place.
From those places the songs of people giving thanks will be
　　heard.
　　The sound of great joy will come from there.
I will cause there to be more of my people.
　　There will not be fewer of them.
I will bring them honor.
　　People will have respect for them.
Things will be as they used to be for Jacob's people.
　　I will make their community firm and secure.
　　I will punish everyone who treats them badly.
Their leader will be one of their own people.
　　Their ruler will rise up from among them.

I will bring him near.
> And he will come close to me.
> He will commit himself to serve me,"
> announces the LORD.
"So you will be my people.
> And I will be your God."

"At that time I will be the God of all the families of Israel," announces the LORD. "And they will be my people."
The LORD says,

"Some of my people will live through
> everything their enemies do to them.
They will find help in the desert.
> I will come to give peace and rest to Israel."

The LORD appeared to us in the past. He said,

"I have loved you with a love that lasts forever.
> I have kept on loving you with a kindness that never fails.
I will build you up again.
> Nation of Israel, you will be rebuilt.
Once again you will use your tambourines to celebrate.
> You will go out and dance with joy.
Once again you will plant vineyards
> on the hills of Samaria.
Farmers will plant them.
> They will enjoy their fruit.
There will be a day when those on guard duty will cry out.
> They will stand on the hills of Ephraim.
> And they will shout,
'Come! Let's go up to Zion.
> Let's go up to where the LORD our God is.'"

remember what you read

1. What is something you noticed for the first time?

_____

_____

_____

_____

2. What questions did you have?

_____

_____

_____

_____

3. Was there anything that bothered you?

_____

_____

_____

_____

4. What did you learn about loving God?

_____

_____

_____

_____

5. What did you learn about loving others?

_____

_____

_____

_____

JEREMIAH, PART 7

introduction to Jeremiah, part 7

Jeremiah continues to tell the people how angry God is with them. But God also promised to bring back the people. Again we see a prediction of a future king, a "godly Branch," who would rule according to God's covenant agreement with Israel.

The LORD says,

"Sing for joy because the people of Jacob are blessed.
Shout because the LORD has made them the greatest nation.
Make your praises heard.
Say, 'LORD, save your people.
Save the people who are left alive in Israel.'

Then young women will dance and be glad.
And so will the men, young and old alike.
I will turn their mourning into gladness.
I will comfort them.
And I will give them joy instead of sorrow.
I will satisfy the priests. I will give them more than enough.
And my people will be filled with the good things I give them,"
announces the LORD.

The LORD says,

"A voice is heard in Ramah.
It is the sound of weeping and deep sadness.

Rachel is weeping for her children.
    She refuses to be comforted,
    because they are gone."

The LORD says,

"Do not weep anymore.
    Do not let tears fall from your eyes.
I will reward you for your work,"
    announces the LORD.
    "Your children will return from the land of the enemy.
So there is hope for your children,"
    announces the LORD.

"The days are coming," announces the LORD.
    "I will make a new covenant
with the people of Israel.
    I will also make it with the people of Judah.
It will not be like the covenant
    I made with their people of long ago.
That was when I took them by the hand.
    I led them out of Egypt.
But they broke my covenant.
    They did it even though I was like a husband to them,"
    announces the LORD.
"This is the covenant I will make with Israel
    after that time," announces the LORD.
"I will put my law in their minds.
    I will write it on their hearts.
I will be their God.
    And they will be my people.
They will not need to teach their neighbor anymore.
    And they will not need to teach one another anymore.
    They will not need to say, 'Know the LORD.'
That's because everyone will know me.
    From the least important of them to the most important,
    all of them will know me,"
    announces the LORD.

"I will forgive their evil ways.
   I will not remember their sins anymore."

The LORD speaks.

He makes the sun
   shine by day.
He orders the moon and stars
   to shine at night.
He stirs up the ocean.
   He makes its waves roar.
   His name is the LORD Who Rules Over All.
"Suppose my orders for creation disappear from my sight,"
   announces the LORD.
"Only then will the people of Israel stop being
   a nation in my sight."

The LORD says,

"Suppose the sky above could be measured.
   Suppose the foundations of the earth below could be
      completely discovered.
Only then would I turn away the people of Israel.
   Even though they have committed many sins,
   I will still accept them,"
   announces the LORD.

"The days are coming," announces the LORD. "At that time Jerusalem will be rebuilt for me. The city will never again be pulled up by the roots. It will never be destroyed."

A message from the LORD came to Jeremiah. It came in the 10th year that Zedekiah was king of Judah. It was in the 18th year of the rule of Nebuchadnezzar. The armies of the king of Babylon were getting ready to attack Jerusalem. Jeremiah the prophet was being held as a prisoner. He was kept in the courtyard of the guard. It was part of Judah's royal palace.

Zedekiah, the king of Judah, had made Jeremiah a prisoner there. Zedekiah had said to him, "Why do you prophesy as you do? You say, 'The LORD says, "I am about to hand over this city to the king of Babylon. He will capture it. Zedekiah, the king of Judah, will not escape from the powerful hands of the armies of Babylon. He will certainly be handed over to the king of Babylon. Zedekiah will speak with him face to face. He will see him with his own eyes. Nebuchadnezzar will take Zedekiah to Babylon. Zedekiah will remain there until I deal with him," announces the LORD. "Suppose you fight against the armies of Babylon. If you do, you will not succeed." ' "

The LORD says, "I have brought all this horrible trouble on these people. But now I will give them all the good things I have promised them. Once more fields will be bought in this land. It is the land about which you now say, 'It is a dry and empty desert. It doesn't have any people or animals in it. It has been handed over to the armies of Babylon.' Fields will be bought with silver. Deeds will be signed, sealed and witnessed. That will be done in the territory of Benjamin. It will be done in the villages around Jerusalem and in the towns of Judah. It will also be done in the towns of the central hill country. And it will be done in the towns of the western hills and the Negev Desert. I will bless their people with great success again," announces the LORD.

Jeremiah was still being held as a prisoner. He was kept in the courtyard of the guard. Then another message from the LORD came to him. The LORD said, "I made the earth. I formed it. And I set it in place. The LORD is my name. Call out to me. I will answer you. I will tell you great things you do not know. And unless I do, you wouldn't be able to find out about them." The LORD is the God of Israel. He speaks about the houses in Jerusalem. He talks about the royal palaces of Judah. The people had torn down many of them. They had used their stones to strengthen the city walls against attack. That was during their fight with the armies of Babylon. The LORD says, "The houses will be filled with dead bodies.

They will be the bodies of the people I will kill. I will kill them when I am very angry with them. I will hide my face from this city. That's because its people have committed so many sins.

"But now I will bring health and healing to Jerusalem. I will heal my people. I will let them enjoy great peace and security. I will bring Judah and Israel back from the places where they have been taken. I will build up the nation again. It will be just as it was before. I will wash from its people all the sins they have committed against me. And I will forgive all the sins they committed when they turned away from me. Then this city will bring me fame, joy, praise and honor. All the nations on earth will hear about the good things I do for this city. They will see the great success and peace I give it. Then they will be filled with wonder. And they will tremble with fear."

The Lord says, "You say about this place, 'It's a dry and empty desert. It doesn't have any people or animals in it.' The towns of Judah and the streets of Jerusalem are now deserted. So they do not have any people or animals living in them. But happy sounds will be heard there once more. They will be the sounds of joy and gladness. The voices of brides and grooms will fill the streets. And the voices of those who bring thank offerings to my house will be heard there. They will say,

" 'Give thanks to the Lord who rules over all,
   because he is good.
   His faithful love continues forever.'

That's because I will bless this land with great success again. It will be as it was before," says the Lord.

The Lord who rules over all says, "This place is a desert. It does not have any people or animals in it. But there will again be grasslands near all its towns. Shepherds will rest their flocks there. Flocks will again pass under the hands of shepherds as they count their sheep," says the Lord. "That will be done in the towns of the central hill country. It will be done in the western hills and the Negev Desert. It will be done in the territory of Benjamin. And it will be done in the villages around Jerusalem and in the towns of Judah.

"The days are coming," announces the LORD. "At that time I will fulfill my good promise to my people. I made it to the people of Israel and Judah.

"Here is what I will do in those days and at that time.
I will make a godly Branch grow from David's royal line.
He will do what is fair and right in the land.
In those days Judah will be saved.
Jerusalem will live in safety.
And it will be called
The LORD Who Makes Us Right With Himself.'"

The LORD says, "David will always have a son to sit on the throne of Israel. The priests, who are Levites, will always have a man to serve me. He will sacrifice burnt offerings. He will burn grain offerings. And he will offer sacrifices."

A message from the LORD came to Jeremiah. The LORD said, "Haven't you noticed what these people are saying? They say, 'The LORD once chose the two kingdoms of Israel and Judah. But now he has turned his back on them.' So they hate my people. They do not think of them as a nation anymore. I say, 'What if I had not made my covenant with day and night? What if I had not established the laws of heaven and earth? Only then would I turn my back on the children of Jacob and my servant David. Only then would I not choose one of David's sons to rule over the children of Abraham, Isaac and Jacob. But I will bless my people with great success again. I will love them with tender love.'"

remember what you read

1. What is something you noticed for the first time?

_____

_____

_____

_____

2. What questions did you have?

_____

_____

_____

_____

3. Was there anything that bothered you?

_____

_____

_____

_____

4. What did you learn about loving God?

_____

_____

_____

_____

5. What did you learn about loving others?

_____

_____

_____

_____

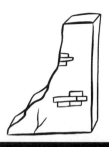

JEREMIAH, PART 8

introduction to Jeremiah, part 8

In today's reading, Jeremiah tells about the last days of the nation of Judah. He tells how the Babylonians destroyed Jerusalem.

A message from the LORD came to Jeremiah. King Zedekiah had made a covenant with all the people in Jerusalem. He had told them to set their Hebrew slaves free. All of them had to do this. That applied to male and female slaves alike. No one was allowed to hold another Hebrew as a slave. So all the officials and people entered into this covenant. They agreed to set their male and female slaves free. They agreed not to hold them as slaves anymore. Instead, they set them free. But later they changed their minds. They took back the people they had set free. They made them slaves again.

Then a message from the LORD came to Jeremiah. The LORD is the God of Israel. He says, "I made a covenant with your people of long ago. I brought them out of Egypt. That is the land where they were slaves. I said, 'Every seventh year you must set your people free. Each of you must set free all the Hebrews who have sold themselves to you. Let them serve you for six years. Then you must let them go free.' But your people of long ago did not listen to me. They did not pay any attention to me. Recently you turned away from your sins. You did what is right in my eyes. Each of you set your Hebrew slaves free. You even made a covenant in front of me. You did it in the house where I have put my Name. But now you have turned around. You have treated my name as if it were not holy. Each of you has taken back your male and female slaves. You had set them free to go where they wished. But now you have forced them to become your slaves again."

So the LORD says, "You have not obeyed me. You have not set your Hebrew slaves free. So now I will set you free," announces the LORD. "I will set you free to be destroyed by war, plague and hunger. I will make all the kingdoms on earth displeased with you. Those people who have broken my covenant will be punished. They have not lived up to the terms of the covenant they made in front of me. When you made that covenant, you cut a calf in two. Then you walked between its pieces. Now I will cut you to pieces. That includes all of you who walked between the pieces of the calf. It includes the leaders of Judah and Jerusalem, the court officials and the priests. It also includes some of the people of the land. So I will hand over all those people to their enemies who want to kill them. Their dead bodies will become food for the birds and the wild animals.

"I will hand over King Zedekiah and his officials to their enemies. I will hand them over to those who want to kill them. I will hand them over to the armies of the king of Babylon. They have now pulled back from you. But I am going to give an order," announces the LORD. "I will bring them back to this city. They will fight against it. They will capture it and burn it down. And I will completely destroy the towns of Judah. No one will be able to live there."

༄

Nebuchadnezzar, the king of Babylon, appointed Zedekiah to be king of Judah. He was the son of Josiah. Zedekiah ruled in place of Jehoiachin, the son of Jehoiakim. Zedekiah and his attendants didn't pay any attention to what the LORD had said through Jeremiah the prophet. And the people of the land didn't pay any attention either.

But King Zedekiah sent Jehukal to Jeremiah the prophet. He said, "Please pray to the LORD our God for us."

At that time Jeremiah was free to come and go among the people.

Jeremiah had not yet been put in prison. The armies of Babylon were attacking Jerusalem. They received a report that Pharaoh's army had marched out of Egypt to help Zedekiah. So armies of Babylon pulled back from Jerusalem.

A message from the LORD came to Jeremiah. The LORD is the God of Israel. He says, "The king of Judah has sent you to ask me for advice. Tell him, 'Pharaoh's army has marched out to help you. But it will go back to its own land. It will return to Egypt. Then the armies of Babylon will come back here. They will attack this city. They will capture it. Then they will burn it down.'

Shephatiah, Gedaliah, Jehukal and Pashhur heard what Jeremiah was telling all the people. "The LORD says, 'Those who stay in this city will die of war, hunger or plague. But those who go over to the side of the Babylonians will live. They will escape with their lives. They will remain alive.' The LORD also says, 'This city will certainly be handed over to the armies of the king of Babylon. They will capture it.'"

Then these officials said to the king, "This man should be put to death. What he says is making the soldiers who are left in this city lose hope. It's making all the people lose hope too. He isn't interested in what is best for the people. In fact, he's trying to destroy them."

"He's in your hands," King Zedekiah answered. "I can't do anything to oppose you."

So they took Jeremiah and put him into an empty well. It didn't have any water in it. All it had was mud. And Jeremiah sank down into the mud.

Ebed-Melek was an official in the royal palace. He was from the land of Cush. He heard that Jeremiah had been put into the well. The king was sitting by the Benjamin Gate at that time. Ebed-Melek went out of the palace. He said to the king, "My king and master, everything these men have done to Jeremiah the prophet is evil. They have thrown him into an empty well. Soon there won't be any more bread in the city. Then he'll starve to death."

So the king gave an order to Ebed-Melek the Cushite. He said, "Take with you 30 men from here. Lift Jeremiah the prophet out of the well before he dies."

Then Ebed-Melek took the men with him. He went to a room in the palace. It was under the place where the treasures were stored. He got some old rags and worn-out clothes from there. Then he let them down with ropes to Jeremiah in the well. Ebed-Melek the Cushite told Jeremiah what to do. Ebed-Melek said, "Put these old rags and worn-out clothes under your arms. They'll pad the ropes." So Jeremiah did. Then the men pulled him up with the ropes. They lifted him out of the well. And Jeremiah remained in the courtyard of the guard.

∽〭〬〬〬

Here is how Jerusalem was captured. Nebuchadnezzar, the king of Babylon, marched out against Jerusalem. He came with all his armies and attacked it. It was in the ninth year that Zedekiah was king of Judah. It was in the tenth month. The city wall was broken through. It happened on the ninth day of the fourth month. It was in the 11th year of Zedekiah's rule. All the officials of the king of Babylon came. King Zedekiah and all the soldiers saw them. Then they ran away. They left the city at night. They went by way of the king's garden. They went out through the gate between the two walls. And they headed toward the Arabah Valley.

But the armies of Babylon chased them. They caught up with Zedekiah in the plains near Jericho. They captured him there. And they took him to Nebuchadnezzar, the king of Babylon. He was at Riblah in the land of Hamath. That's where Nebuchadnezzar decided how Zedekiah would be punished. The king of Babylon killed the sons of Zedekiah at Riblah. He forced Zedekiah to watch it with his own eyes. He also killed all the nobles of Judah. Then he poked out Zedekiah's eyes. He put him in bronze chains. And he took him to Babylon.

The Babylonians set the royal palace on fire. They also set fire to the houses of the people. And they broke down the walls of Jerusalem. Nebuzaradan was commander of the royal guard. Some people still remained in the city. But he took them away to Babylon as prisoners. He also took along those who had gone over to his side. And he took the rest of the people. Nebuzaradan, the commander of the guard, left some of the poor people of Judah behind. They didn't own anything. So at that time he gave them vineyards and fields.

Nebuchadnezzar, the king of Babylon, had given orders about Jeremiah. He had given them to Nebuzaradan, the commander of the royal guard. Nebuchadnezzar had said, "Take him. Look after him. Don't harm him. Do for him anything he asks." They sent for Jeremiah. They had him taken out of the courtyard of the guard. They turned him over to Gedaliah. Gedaliah was the son of Ahikam, the son of Shaphan. They told Gedaliah to take Jeremiah back to his home. So Jeremiah remained among his own people.

∽♉♉∾

A message from the LORD came to Jeremiah. It came while he was being kept in the courtyard of the guard. The LORD said, "Go. Speak to Ebed-Melek the Cushite. Tell him, 'The LORD who rules over all is the God of Israel. He says, "I am about to make the words I spoke against this city come true. I will not give success to it. Instead, I will bring horrible trouble on it. At that time my words will come true. You will see it with your own eyes. But I will save you on that day," announces the LORD. "You will not be handed over to those you are afraid of. I will save you. You will not be killed by a sword. Instead, you will escape with your life. That's because you trust in me," announces the LORD.'"

remember what you read

1. What is something you noticed for the first time?

_____

_____

_____

_____

2. What questions did you have?

_____

_____

_____

_____

3. Was there anything that bothered you?

_____

_____

_____

_____

4. What did you learn about loving God?

_____

_____

_____

_____

5. What did you learn about loving others?

_____

_____

_____

_____

introduction to Jeremiah, part 9

Today's reading begins with what happened after the Babylonians destroyed Jerusalem.

The final big section of Jeremiah talks about the nations around Judah. Jeremiah spoke these prophecies over many years.

༄ᢒᢒᢒᢇ

Jeremiah was among all the prisoners from Jerusalem and Judah. They were being taken to Babylon. But the commander of the guard found Jeremiah. The commander said to him, "The LORD your God ordered that this place be destroyed. And now he has brought it about. He has done exactly what he said he would do. All these things have happened because you people sinned against the LORD. You didn't obey him. But today I'm setting you free from the chains on your wrists. Come with me to Babylon if you want to. I'll take good care of you there. But if you don't want to come, then don't. The whole country lies in front of you. Go anywhere you want to." But before Jeremiah turned to go, Nebuzaradan continued, "Go back to Gedaliah, the son of Ahikam. The king of Babylon has appointed Gedaliah to be over the towns of Judah. Go and live with him among your people. Or go anywhere else you want to." Ahikam was the son of Shaphan.

The commander gave Jeremiah food and water. He also gave him a gift. Then he let Jeremiah go. So Jeremiah went to Mizpah to see Gedaliah, the son of Ahikam. Jeremiah stayed with him. Jeremiah lived among the people who were left behind in the land.

ᏯᏯᏯᎧ

In the seventh month Ishmael came with ten men to Gedaliah, the son of Ahikam, at Mizpah. He had been one of the king's officers. Ishmael and his ten men were eating together at Mizpah. They got up and struck down Gedaliah, the son of Ahikam, with their swords. They killed him even though the king of Babylon had appointed him as governor over Judah. Ishmael also killed all the men of Judah who were with Gedaliah at Mizpah. And he killed the Babylonian soldiers who were there.

ᏯᏯᏯᎧ

Then all the army officers approached Jeremiah. All the people from the least important of them to the most important also came. All of them said to Jeremiah the prophet, "Please listen to our appeal. Pray to the LORD your God. Pray for all of us who are left here. Once there were many of us. But as you can see, only a few of us are left now. So pray to the LORD your God. Pray that he'll tell us where we should go. Pray that he'll tell us what we should do."

"I've heard you," Jeremiah the prophet replied. "I'll certainly pray to the LORD your God. I'll do what you have asked me to do. In fact, I'll tell you everything the LORD says. I won't keep anything back from you."

Then they said to Jeremiah, "We'll do everything the LORD your God sends you to tell us to do. If we don't, may he be a true and faithful witness against us. It doesn't matter whether what you say is in our favor or not. We're asking you to pray to the LORD our God. And we'll obey him. Things will go well with us. That's because we will obey the LORD our God."

Ten days later a message came to Jeremiah from the LORD. So Jeremiah sent for Johanan, the son of Kareah, and all the other army officers with him. He said to all of them, "The LORD is the God of Israel. You asked me to present your appeal to him. He told me, 'Stay in this land. Then I will build you up. I will not tear you down. I will plant you. I will not pull you up by the roots. I have

decided to stop bringing trouble on you. Do not be afraid of the
king of Babylon. You are afraid of him now. Do not be,' announces
the Lord. 'I am with you. I will keep you safe. I will save you from
his power. I will show you my loving concern. Then he will have
concern for you. And he will let you return to your land.'

Jeremiah finished telling the people everything the Lord their
God had said. Jeremiah told them everything the Lord had sent
him to tell them. After that, Azariah, the son of Hoshaiah, and
Johanan, the son of Kareah, spoke to Jeremiah. And all the proud
men joined them. They said, "You are lying! The Lord our God
hasn't sent you to speak to us. He hasn't told you to say, 'You must
not go to Egypt and make your homes there.' But Baruch, the son
of Neriah, is turning you against us. He wants us to be handed over
to the Babylonians. Then they can kill us. Or they can take us away
to Babylon."

So Johanan, the son of Kareah, disobeyed the Lord's command.
So did all the other army officers and all the people. They didn't
stay in the land of Judah. So the Jewish leaders disobeyed the Lord.
They took everyone to Egypt. They went all the way to Tahpanhes.

∽♊♊〜

In Tahpanhes a message from the Lord came to Jeremiah. The
Lord said, "Make sure the Jews are watching you. Then get some
large stones. Go to the entrance to Pharaoh's house in Tahpanhes.
Bury the stones in the clay under the brick walkway there. Then
tell the Jews, 'The Lord who rules over all is the God of Israel. He
says, "I will send for my servant Nebuchadnezzar, the king of Babylon. And I will set his throne over these stones that are buried
here. He will set up his royal tent over them. He will come and
attack Egypt. He will bring death to those I have appointed to die.
He will take away as prisoners those I have appointed to be tak-
en away. And he will kill with swords those I have appointed to
be killed. He will set the temples of the gods of Egypt on fire. He
will burn down their temples. He will take away the statues of
their gods. Nebuchadnezzar will be like a shepherd who picks his
coat clean of lice. Nebuchadnezzar will pick Egypt clean and then

depart. At Heliopolis in Egypt he will smash the sacred pillars to pieces. And he will burn down the temples of the gods of Egypt." ' "

✺

Jeremiah talked to Baruch, the son of Neriah. It was in the fourth year that Jehoiakim, the son of Josiah, was king of Judah. It was when Baruch had written down on a scroll the words Jeremiah the prophet told him to write. Jeremiah had said, "The Lord is the God of Israel. Baruch, he says to you, 'You have said, "How terrible it is for me! The Lord has added sorrow to my pain. I'm worn out from all my groaning. I can't find any rest." ' But here is what the Lord has told me to say to you, Baruch. 'The Lord says, "I will destroy what I have built up. I will pull up by the roots what I have planted. I will do this throughout the earth. So should you seek great things for yourself? Do not seek them. I will bring trouble on everyone," announces the Lord. "But no matter where you go, I will let you escape with your life." ' "

✺

A message from the Lord came to Jeremiah the prophet. It was about the nations.

Here is what the Lord says about Egypt.

Here is his message against the army of Pharaoh Necho. He was king of Egypt. Nebuchadnezzar, the king of Babylon, won the battle over Necho's army. That happened at Carchemish on the Euphrates River. It was in the fourth year that Jehoiakim was king of Judah. He was the son of Josiah. The message says,

"Egyptians, prepare your shields!
   Prepare large and small shields alike!
   March out for battle!
Get the horses and chariots ready to ride!
   Take up your battle positions!
   Put on your helmets!
Shine up your spears!
   Put on your armor!

What do I see?
The Egyptians are terrified.
They are pulling back.
Their soldiers are losing.
They run away as fast as they can.
They do not look back.
There is terror on every side," announces the LORD.
"Those who run fast can't get away.
Those who are strong can't escape.
In the north by the Euphrates River
they trip and fall.

⟨ornament⟩

Nebuchadnezzar, the king of Babylon, was coming to attack Egypt. Here is the message the LORD spoke to Jeremiah the prophet about it. He said,

"Egyptians, here is what I want you to announce in your
land.
Announce it in the city of Migdol.
Also announce it in Memphis and Tahpanhes.
Say, 'Take up your battle positions! Get ready!
The sword eats up those around you.'
Why are your soldiers lying on the ground?
They can't stand, because I bring them down.
They will trip again and again.
They will fall over one another.
They will say, 'Get up. Let's go back home.
Let's return to our own people and our own lands.
Let's get away from the swords
that will bring us great harm.'
The Egyptian soldiers will cry out,
'Pharaoh, our king, is only a loud noise.
He has missed his chance to win the battle.'

The LORD who rules over all is the God of Israel. He says, "I am about to punish Amon, the god of Thebes. I will also punish

Pharaoh. I will punish Egypt and its gods and kings. And I will punish those who depend on Pharaoh. I will hand them over to those who want to kill them. I will give them to Nebuchadnezzar, the king of Babylon, and his officers. But later, many people will live in Egypt again as in times past," announces the LORD.

"People of Jacob, do not be afraid.
    You are my servant.
    Israel, do not be terrified.
I will bring you safely out of a place far away.
    I will bring your children back
    from the land where they were taken.
Your people will have peace and security again.
    And no one will make them afraid.
People of Jacob, do not be afraid.
    You are my servant.
    I am with you,"
    announces the LORD.
"I will completely destroy all the nations
    among which I scatter you.
    But I will not completely destroy you.
I will correct you. But I will be fair.
    I will not let you go without any punishment."

remember what you read

1. What is something you noticed for the first time?

_____

_____

_____

_____

2. What questions did you have?

_____

_____

_____

_____

3. Was there anything that bothered you?

_____

_____

_____

_____

4. What did you learn about loving God?

_____

_____

_____

_____

5. What did you learn about loving others?

_____

_____

_____

_____

JEREMIAH, PART 10

introduction to Jeremiah, part 10

Today's reading finishes the final big section of Jeremiah where he talks about the nations around Judah. He ends with a prophecy against Babylon, the empire that brought God's judgment on all these nations. Jeremiah spoke these prophecies over many years.

A message from the LORD came to Jeremiah the prophet. It was about the Philistines before Pharaoh attacked the city of Gaza. The LORD said,

"The armies of Babylon are like waters rising in the north.
    They will become a great flood.
They will flow over the land and everything in it.
    They will flow over the towns and those who live in
        them.
The people will cry out.
    All those who live in the land will weep.
They will weep when they hear galloping horses.
    They will weep at the noise of enemy chariots.
    They will weep at the rumble of their wheels.
Parents will not even try to help their children.
    Their hands will not be able to help them.
The day has come
    to destroy all the Philistines.
The time has come to remove all those
    who could help Tyre and Sidon.

I am about to destroy the Philistines.
    I will not leave anyone alive
    who came from the coasts of Crete.

∽၇၇၃∼

Here is what the LORD says about Moab.

The LORD who rules over all is the God of Israel. He says,

"Moab has been at peace and rest from its earliest days.
    It is like wine that has not been shaken up.
It has not been poured from one jar to another.
    Moab's people have not been taken away from their land.
They are like wine that tastes as it always did.
    Its smell has not changed at all.
But other days are coming," announces the LORD.
"At that time I will send people who pour wine from pitchers.
    They will pour Moab out like wine.
They will empty its pitchers.
    They will smash its jars.
Then Moab's people will be ashamed of their god named
        Chemosh.
    They will be ashamed just as the people of Israel were
    when they trusted in their false god at Bethel.

"We have heard all about Moab's pride.
    We have heard how very proud they are.
They think they are so much better than others.
    Their pride reaches deep down inside their hearts.
I know how rude they are.
    But it will not get them anywhere," announces the LORD.
    "Their bragging does not accomplish anything.
So I weep over Moab.
    I cry for all Moab's people.
    I groan for the people of Kir Hareseth.

"How broken Moab is! How the people weep!
    They turn away from others
    because they are so ashamed.

All those around them laugh at them.
They are shocked at them."

The LORD says,

"Look! Nebuchadnezzar is like an eagle diving down.
He is spreading his wings over Moab.
Moab will be destroyed as a nation.
That is because its people thought
they were better than the LORD.
You people of Moab,"
announces the LORD,
"terror, a pit and a trap are waiting for you.
Anyone who runs away from the terror
will fall into the pit.
Anyone who climbs out of the pit
will be caught in the trap.
The time is coming
when I will punish Moab,"
announces the LORD.

"But in days to come
I will bless Moab with great success again,"
announces the LORD.

This ends the report about how the LORD would judge Moab.

Here is what the LORD says about the people of Ammon.
He says,

"Doesn't Israel have any sons?
Doesn't Israel have anyone
to take over the family property?
Then why has the god named Molek taken over Gad?
Why do those who worship him live in its towns?
But a new day is coming,"
announces the LORD.

"At that time I will sound the battle cry.
    I will sound it against Rabbah in the land of Ammon.
It will become a pile of broken-down buildings.
    The villages around it will be set on fire.
Then Israel will drive out
    those who drove her out,"
    says the Lord.
"Heshbon, weep for Ai! It is destroyed!
    Cry out, you who live in Rabbah!
Put on the clothes of sadness and mourn.
    Run here and there inside the walls.
Your god named Molek will be carried away.
    So will its priests and officials.
Why do you brag about your valleys?
    You brag that they produce so many crops.
Ammon, you are an unfaithful country.
    You trust in your riches. You say,
    'Who will attack me?'
I will bring terror on you.
    It will come from all those around you,"
    announces the Lord. He is the Lord who rules
        over all.
"Every one of you will be driven away.
    No one will bring back those who escape.

"But after that, I will bless the people of Ammon
    with great success again,"
    announces the Lord.

Here is what the Lord says about Edom.

I've heard a message from the Lord.
    A messenger was sent to the nations. The Lord told him to
        say,
"Gather yourselves together to attack Edom!
    Prepare for battle!"

The LORD says to Edom, "I will make you weak among
 the nations.
 They will hate you.
You live in the safety of the rocks.
 You live on top of the hills.
But the terror you stir up has now turned against
 you.
 Your proud heart has tricked you.
You build your nest as high as an eagle does.
 But I will bring you down from there,"
 announces the LORD.
"People of Edom,
 all those who pass by you will be shocked.
They will make fun of you
 because of all your wounds.
Sodom and Gomorrah were destroyed.
 So were the towns that were near them,"
 says the LORD.
"You will be just like them.
 No one will live in your land.
 No human beings will stay there.

✺

Here is what the LORD says about Damascus. He says,

"The people of Hamath and Arpad are terrified.
 They have heard bad news.
They have lost all hope.
 They are troubled like the rolling sea.
The people of Damascus have become weak.
 They have turned to run away.
 Panic has taken hold of them.
Suffering and pain have taken hold of them.
 Their pain is like the pain of a woman having a baby.
Why hasn't the famous city been deserted?
 It is the town I take delight in.

You can be sure its young men will fall dead in the streets.
　All its soldiers will be put to death at that time,"
　announces the LORD who rules over all.
"I will set the walls of Damascus on fire.
　It will burn down the strong towers of King Ben-Hadad."

∽⟋⟋∾

Here is what the LORD says about the people of Kedar and the kingdoms of Hazor. Nebuchadnezzar, the king of Babylon, was planning to attack them.

"Armies of Babylon, prepare for battle.
Attack a nation that feels secure.
　Its people do not have any worries,"
　announces the LORD.
"That nation does not have gates or bars that lock them.
　Its people live far from danger.
Their camels will be stolen.
　Their large herds will be taken away.
I will scatter to the winds those who are in places far away.
　I will bring trouble on them from every side,"
　announces the LORD.
"Hazor will become a home for wild dogs.
　It will be a dry and empty desert forever.
No one will live in that land.
　No human beings will stay there."

∽⟋⟋∾

A message from the LORD came to Jeremiah the prophet. It was about Elam. It came shortly after Zedekiah became king of Judah. The LORD who rules over all said,

"Elam's bow is the secret of its strength.
　But I will break it.
I will bring the four winds against Elam.
　I will bring them from all four directions.

I will scatter Elam's people to the four winds.
   They will be taken away
   to every nation on earth.
I will use Elam's enemies to smash them.
   Those who want to kill them will kill them.
I will bring trouble on Elam's people.
   My anger will be great against them,"
   announces the LORD.
"I will chase them with swords.
   I will hunt them down
   until I have destroyed them.
I will set up my throne in Elam.
   I will destroy its king and officials,"
   announces the LORD.

"But in days to come I will bless Elam
   with great success again,"
   announces the LORD.

remember what you read

1. What is something you noticed for the first time?

_____

_____

_____

_____

2. What questions did you have?

_____

_____

_____

_____

3. Was there anything that bothered you?

_____

_____

_____

_____

4. What did you learn about loving God?

_____

_____

_____

_____

5. What did you learn about loving others?

_____

_____

_____

_____

introduction to Jeremiah, part II

Today's reading finishes the final big section of Jeremiah where he talks about the nations around Judah. He ends with a prophecy against Babylon, the empire that brought God's judgment on all these nations. Jeremiah spoke these prophecies over many years.

Here is the message the LORD spoke through Jeremiah the prophet. It was about the city of Babylon and the land of Babylon. He said,

"Announce this message among the nations.
  Lift up a banner.
Let the nations hear the message.
  Do not keep anything back.
Say, 'Babylon will be captured.
  The god named Bel will be put to shame.
  The god named Marduk will be filled with terror.
Babylon's gods will be put to shame.
  The gods its people made will be filled with terror.'
A nation from the north will attack it.
  That nation will destroy Babylon.
No one will live there.
  People and animals alike will run away.

"The days are coming,"
  announces the LORD.

"At that time the people of Israel and Judah will gather
together.
  They will come in tears to me.
  I am the LORD their God.
They will ask how to get to Zion.
  Then they will turn their faces toward it.
They will come and join themselves to me.
  They will enter into the covenant I make with them.
It will last forever.
  It will never be forgotten.

"My people have been like lost sheep.
  Their shepherds have led them astray.
  They have caused them to wander in the mountains.
They have wandered over mountains and hills.
  They have forgotten that I am their true resting place.
Everyone who found them destroyed them.
  Their enemies said, 'We aren't guilty.
They sinned against the LORD.
  He gave them everything they needed.
  He has always been Israel's hope.'

"All you who shoot arrows,
  take up your battle positions around Babylon.
Shoot at it! Do not spare any arrows!
  Its people have sinned against me.
Shout against them on every side!
  They are giving up.
The towers of the city are falling.
  Its walls are being pulled down.
The LORD is paying back its people.
  So pay them back yourselves.
  Do to them what they have done to others.
Do not leave anyone in Babylon to plant the fields.
  Do not leave anyone to harvest the grain.
Let each of them return to their own people.
  Let them run away to their own land.
  If they don't, their enemy's sword will bring them great
harm.

"Israel is like a scattered flock
    that lions have chased away.
The first lion that ate them up
    was the king of Assyria.
The last one that broke their bones
    was Nebuchadnezzar, the king of Babylon."

The LORD who rules over all is the God of Israel. He says,

"I punished the king of Assyria.
    In the same way, I will punish
    the king of Babylon and his land.
But I will bring Israel back to their own grasslands.
    I will feed them on Mount Carmel and in Bashan.
I will satisfy their hunger
    on the hills of Ephraim and Gilead.
The days are coming,"
    announces the LORD.
"At that time people will search for Israel's guilt.
    But they will not find any.
They will search for Judah's sins.
    But they will not find any.
    That is because I will forgive the people I have spared.

"Proud Babylonians, I am against you,"
    announces the Lord.
The LORD who rules over all says,
    "Your day to be judged has come.
    It is time for you to be punished.
You proud people will trip and fall.
    No one will help you up.
I will start a fire in your towns.
    It will burn up everyone around you."

The LORD who rules over all says,

"The people of Israel are being treated badly.
    So are the people of Judah.
Those who have captured them are holding them.
    They refuse to let them go.

But I am strong and will save them.
My name is the LORD Who Rules Over All.
I will stand up for them.
I will bring peace and rest to their land.
But I will bring trouble to those who live in Babylon.

The LORD says,

"I used my power to make the earth.
I used my wisdom to set the world in place.
I used my understanding to spread out the heavens.
When I thunder, the waters in the heavens roar.
I make clouds rise from one end of the earth to the other.
I send lightning with the rain.
I bring out the wind from my storerooms.

"No one has any sense.
No one knows anything.
Everyone who works with gold is put to shame
by his wooden gods.
His metal gods are fakes.
They can't even breathe.
They are worthless, and people make fun of them.
When I judge them, they will be destroyed.
But I, the God of Jacob, am not like them.
I give my people everything they need.
I can do this because I made everything, including Israel.
They are the people who belong to me.
My name is the LORD Who Rules Over All.

"Judah, I will pay Babylon back. You will see it with your own eyes. I will pay back all those who live in Babylon. I will pay them back for all the wrong things they have done in Zion," announces the LORD.

"Babylon, I am against you.
Your kingdom is like a destroying mountain.
You have destroyed the whole earth,"
announces the LORD.

"I will reach out my hand against you.
  I will roll you off the cliffs.
  I will make you like a mountain that has been
    burned up.
No rock will be taken from you to be used
  as the most important stone for a building.
No stones will be taken from you
  to be used for a foundation.
Your land will be empty forever,"
  announces the LORD.

"Nations, lift up a banner in the land of Babylon!
  Blow a trumpet among yourselves!
Prepare yourselves for battle against Babylon.
  Send the kingdoms
  of Ararat, Minni and Ashkenaz against it.
Appoint a commander against it.
  Send many horses against it.
  Let them be as many as a huge number of locusts.
Prepare yourselves for battle against Babylon.
  Prepare the kings of the Medes.
Prepare their governors and all their officials.
  Prepare all the countries they rule over.
The Babylonians tremble and shake with fear.
  My plans against them stand firm.
I plan to destroy their land completely.
  Then no one will live there.
Babylon's soldiers have stopped fighting.
  They remain in their forts.
Their strength is all gone.
  They have become weak.
Their buildings are set on fire.
  The metal bars that lock their gates are broken.
One messenger after another
  comes to the king of Babylon.
All of them announce that
  his entire city is captured.

The places where people go across the Euphrates River
     have been captured.
   The swamps have been set on fire.
   And the soldiers are terrified."

The people of Jerusalem say,
"Nebuchadnezzar, the king of Babylon, has destroyed us.
   He has thrown us into a panic.
   He has emptied us out like a jar.
Like a snake he has swallowed us up.
   He has filled his stomach with our rich food.
   Then he has spit us out of his mouth."
The people continue, "May the people of Babylon
   pay for the harmful things they have done to us.
May those who live in Babylon
   pay for spilling the blood of our people."
   That's what the people who live in Zion say.

So the LORD says,

"Come out of there, my people!
   Run for your lives!
   Run away from my great anger.
You will hear about terrible things
   that are happening in Babylon.
   But do not lose hope. Do not be afraid.
You will hear one thing this year.
   And you will hear something else next year.
You will hear about awful things in the land.
   You will hear about one ruler fighting against
      another.
I will punish the gods of Babylon.
   That time will certainly come.
Then the whole land will be full of shame.
   Its people will lie down and die there.
So heaven and earth and everything in them will shout
      for joy.
   They will be glad because of what will happen to Babylon.

Armies will attack it from the north.
　And they will destroy it,"
announces the LORD.

"Babylon's people have killed my people Israel.
　They have also killed people all over the earth.
　So now Babylon itself must fall.
You who have not been killed in the war against Babylon,
　leave! Do not wait!
In a land far away remember me.
　And think about Jerusalem."

The people of Judah reply, "No one honors us anymore.
　People make fun of us.
　Our faces are covered with shame.
People from other lands have entered
　the holy places of the LORD's house."

"But the days are coming," announces the LORD.
　"At that time I will punish the gods of Babylon.
And all through its land
　wounded people will groan.
What if Babylon reached all the way to the heavens?
　What if it made its high walls even stronger?
　I would still send destroyers against it,"
announces the LORD.

〰️

Jeremiah the prophet gave a message to the staff officer Seraiah, the son of Neriah. Neriah was the son of Mahseiah. Jeremiah told Seraiah to take the message with him to Babylon. Seraiah went there with Zedekiah, the king of Judah. He left in the fourth year of Zedekiah's rule. Jeremiah had written about all the trouble that would come on Babylon. He had written it down on a scroll. It included everything that had been recorded about Babylon. Jeremiah said to Seraiah, "When you get to Babylon, here's what I want you to do. Make sure that you read all these words out loud.

Then say, 'LORD, you have said you will destroy this place. You have said that no people or animals will live here. It will be empty forever.' Finish reading the scroll. Tie a stone to it. Throw it into the Euphrates River. Then say, 'In the same way, Babylon will sink down. It will never rise again. That is because I will bring such horrible trouble on it. And its people will fall along with it.'"

remember what you read

1. What is something you noticed for the first time?

_____

_____

_____

_____

2. What questions did you have?

_____

_____

_____

_____

3. Was there anything that bothered you?

_____

_____

_____

_____

4. What did you learn about loving God?

_____

_____

_____

_____

5. What did you learn about loving others?

_____

_____

_____

_____

OBADIAH; EZEKIEL, PART 1

introduction to Obadiah

When Jerusalem was destroyed by the Babylonians, the Edomites didn't do the right thing. They killed people who were running away from Jerusalem. They stole from them. And they were proud and made fun of them. Esau and Jacob were brothers. Esau's descendents were the Edomites. Jacob's descendents were the Israelites. Edom should have treated their family members better.

This is the vision about Edom that Obadiah had.

Here is what the LORD and King says about Edom.

We've heard a message from the LORD.
    A messenger was sent to the nations.
The LORD told him to say,
    "Get up! Let us go and make war against Edom."

The LORD says to Edom,

"I will make you weak among the nations.
    They will look down on you.
You live in the safety of the rocks.
    You make your home high up in the mountains.
    But your proud heart has tricked you.
So you say to yourself,
    'No one can bring me down to the ground.'

You have built your home as high as an eagle does.
    You have made your nest among the stars.
    But I will bring you down from there,"
    announces the LORD.
"Edom, suppose robbers came to you at night.
    They would steal only as much as they wanted.
Suppose grape pickers came to harvest your vines.
    They would still leave a few grapes.
    But you are facing horrible trouble!
People of Esau, everything will be taken away from you.
    Your hidden treasures will be stolen.
All those who are helping you
    will force you to leave your country.
    Your friends will trick you and overpower you.
Those who eat bread with you
    will set a trap for you.
    But you will not see it."

Here is what the LORD announces. "At that time
    I will destroy the wise men of Edom.
I will wipe out the men of understanding
    in the mountains of Esau.
People of Teman, your soldiers will be terrified.
    Everyone in Esau's mountains
    will be cut down by swords.
You did harmful things to the people of Jacob.
    They are your relatives.
So you will be covered with shame.
    You will be destroyed forever.
Outsiders entered the gates of Jerusalem.
    They cast lots to see what each one would get.
Strangers carried off its wealth.
    When that happened, you just stood there and did nothing.
    You were like one of them.
That was a time of trouble for your relatives.
    So you shouldn't have been happy about what happened to
        them.

The people of Judah were destroyed.
  So you should not have been happy about it.
You should not have laughed at them so much
  when they were in trouble.
You should not have marched
  through the gates of my people's city
  when they were in trouble.
You shouldn't have been happy about what happened to
    them.
  You should not have stolen their wealth
  when they were in trouble.
You waited where the roads cross.
  You wanted to cut down those who were running away.
  You should not have done that.
You handed over to their enemies
  those who were still left alive.
You should not have done that.
  They were in trouble.

"The day of the Lord is near
  for all the nations.
Others will do to you
  what you have done to them.
You will be paid back
  for what you have done.
You Edomites made my holy mountain of Zion impure
  by drinking and celebrating there.
So all the nations will drink
  from the cup of my anger.
  And they will keep on drinking from it.
They will vanish.
  It will be as if they had never existed.
But on Mount Zion some of my people will be left alive.
  I will save them.
  Zion will be my holy mountain once again.
And the people of Jacob
  will again receive the land as their own.

They will be like a fire.
  Joseph's people will be like a flame.
The nation of Edom will be like straw.
  Jacob's people will set Edom on fire and burn it up.
No one will be left alive
  among Esau's people."
The Lord has spoken.

Israelites from the Negev Desert
  will take over Esau's mountains.
Israelites from the western hills
  will possess the land of the Philistines.
They'll take over the territories
  of Ephraim and Samaria.
Israelites from the tribe of Benjamin
  will possess the land of Gilead.
Some Israelites were forced to leave their homes.
  They'll come back to Canaan and possess
  it all the way to the town of Zarephath.
Some people from Jerusalem were taken
  to the city of Sepharad.
They'll return and possess
  the towns of the Negev Desert.
Leaders from Mount Zion will go
  and rule over the mountains of Esau.
  And the kingdom will belong to the Lord.

introduction to Ezekiel, part 1

Ezekiel was a priest who was taken to Babylon along with King Jehoiachin. He shares God's words and the visions he saw in three big sections. The first section is warnings to people still in Jerusalem before it was destroyed. The second section is prophecies against other nations. The third section looks ahead to Israel's people returning to their homeland. Ezekiel uses the name Israel for God's people in Babylon, who were from Judah.

I was 30 years old. I was with my people. We had been taken away from our country. We were by the Kebar River in the land of Babylon. On the fifth day of the fourth month, the heavens were opened. I saw visions of God.

I looked up and saw a windstorm coming from the north. I saw a huge cloud. The fire of lightning was flashing out of it. Bright light surrounded it. The center of the fire looked like glowing metal. I saw in the fire something that looked like four living creatures. They appeared to have the shape of a human being. But each of them had four faces and four wings. Their legs were straight. Their feet looked like the feet of a calf. They were as bright as polished bronze. The creatures had human hands under their wings on their four sides. All four of them had faces and wings. The wings of one touched the wings of another. Each of the creatures went straight ahead. They didn't change their direction as they moved.

Here's what their faces looked like. Each of the four creatures had the face of a human being. On the right side each had the face of a lion. On the left each had the face of an ox. Each one also had an eagle's face. That's what their faces looked like. They each had two wings that spread out and lifted up. Each wing touched the wing of another creature on either side. They each had two other wings that covered their bodies. All the creatures went straight ahead. Anywhere their spirits would lead them to go, they would go. They didn't change their direction as they went. The living creatures looked like burning coals of fire or like torches. Fire moved back and forth among the creatures. It was bright. Lightning flashed out of it. The creatures raced back and forth like flashes of lightning.

As I looked at the living creatures, I saw wheels on the ground beside them. Each creature had four faces. Here's how the wheels looked and worked. They gleamed like topaz. All four of them looked alike. Each one seemed to be made like a wheel inside another wheel at right angles. The wheels could go in any one of the four directions the creatures faced. The wheels didn't change their direction as the creatures moved. Their rims were high and terrifying. All four rims were full of eyes all the way around them.

When the living creatures moved, the wheels beside them moved. When the creatures rose from the ground, the wheels also rose. Anywhere their spirits would lead them to go, they would go. And the wheels would rise along with them. That's because the spirits of the living creatures were in the wheels. When the living creatures moved, the wheels also moved. When the creatures stood still, they also stood still. When the creatures rose from the ground, the wheels rose along with them. That's because the spirits of the living creatures were in the wheels.

Something that looked like a huge space was spread out above the heads of the living creatures. It gleamed like crystal. It was terrifying. The wings of the creatures were spread out under the space. They reached out toward one another. Each creature had two wings covering its body. When the living creatures moved, I heard the sound of their wings. It was like the roar of rushing waters. It sounded like the thundering voice of the Mighty God. It was like the loud noise an army makes. When the creatures stood still, they lowered their wings.

Then a voice came from above the huge space over their heads. They stood with their wings lowered. Above the space over their heads was something that looked like a throne made out of lapis lazuli. On the throne high above was a figure that appeared to be a man. From his waist up he looked like glowing metal that was full of fire. From his waist down he looked like fire. Bright light surrounded him. The glow around him looked like a rainbow in the clouds on a rainy day.

That's what the glory of the Lord looked like. When I saw it, I fell with my face toward the ground. Then I heard the voice of someone speaking.

He said to me, "Son of man, stand up on your feet. I will speak to you." As he spoke, the Spirit of the Lord came into me. He raised me to my feet. I heard him speaking to me.

He said, "Son of man, I am sending you to the people of Israel. That nation has refused to obey me. They have turned against me. They and their people of long ago have been against me to this day. The people I am sending you to are very stubborn. Tell them, 'Here is what the Lord and King says.' They might listen, or they might not. After all, they refuse to obey me. But whether they listen or not, they will know that a prophet was among them. Son of man, do not be afraid of them or of what they say. Do not be afraid, even if thorns and bushes are all around you. Do not be afraid, even if you live among scorpions. Son of man, listen to what I tell you. Do not be like those who refuse to obey me. Open your mouth. Eat what I give you."

Then I looked up. I saw a hand reach out to me. A scroll was in it. He unrolled it in front of me. Both sides had words written on them. They spoke about sadness, sorrow and trouble.

Then he said to me, "Son of man, eat this scroll I am giving you. Fill your stomach with it." So I ate it. And it tasted as sweet as honey in my mouth.

Then he said to me, "Son of man, go to the people of Israel. Give them my message. I am not sending you to people who speak another language that is hard to learn. Instead, I am sending you to the people of Israel. You are not being sent to many nations whose people speak other languages that are hard to learn. You would not be able to understand them. Suppose I had sent you to them. Then they certainly would have listened to you. But the people of Israel do not want to listen to you. That is because they do not want to listen to me. All the Israelites are very stubborn. But I will make you just as stubborn as they are. I will make you very brave. So do not be afraid of them. Do not let them terrify you, even though they refuse to obey me."

Then the Spirit lifted me up and took me away. My spirit was bitter. I was very angry. The power of the LORD was on me. I came to my people who had been brought as prisoners to Tel Aviv. It was near the Kebar River. I went to where they were living. There I sat among them for seven days. I was very sad and scared about everything that had happened.

remember what you read

1. What is something you noticed for the first time?

_____

_____

_____

_____

2. What questions did you have?

_____

_____

_____

_____

3. Was there anything that bothered you?

_____

_____

_____

_____

4. What did you learn about loving God?

_____

_____

_____

_____

5. What did you learn about loving others?

_____

_____

_____

_____

EZEKIEL, PART 2

introduction to Ezekiel, part 2

God took Ezekiel from his place in Babylon and showed him a vision of how evil the people in Jerusalem were. He told him how the proud and wicked leaders and people would be destroyed. But he also promised that he would give his people a new spirit. He would remove their stubborn hearts and give them obedient hearts.

After seven days, a message from the LORD came to me. The LORD said, "Son of man, I have appointed you as a prophet to warn the people of Israel. So listen to my message. Give them a warning from me. Suppose I say to a sinful person, 'You can be sure you will die.' And you do not warn them. You do not try to get them to change their evil ways in order to save their life. Then that sinful person will die because they have sinned. And I will hold you responsible for their death. But suppose you do warn that sinful person. And they do not turn away from their sin or their evil ways. Then they will die because they have sinned. But you will have saved yourself.

"Or suppose a godly person turns away from their godliness and does what is evil. And suppose I put something in their way that will trip them up. Then they will die. Since you did not warn them, they will die for their sin. The godly things that person did will not be remembered. And I will hold you responsible for their death. But suppose you do warn a godly person not to sin. And they do not sin. Then you can be sure that they will live because they listened to your warning. And you will have saved yourself."

The power of the LORD was on me. He said, "Get up. Go out to the plain. I will speak to you there." So I got up and went out to the plain. The glory of the LORD was standing there. It was just like the glory I had seen by the Kebar River. So I fell with my face toward the ground.

Then the Spirit of the LORD came into me. He raised me to my feet. He said to me, "Go, son of man. Shut yourself inside your house. Some people will tie you up with ropes. So you will not be able to go out among your people. I will make your tongue stick to the roof of your mouth. Then you will be silent. You will not be able to correct them. That's because they always refuse to obey me. But later I will speak to you. I will open your mouth. Then you will tell them, 'Here is what the LORD and King says.' Those who listen will listen. And those who refuse to listen will refuse. They always refuse to obey me.

"Son of man, get a block of clay. Put it in front of you. Draw the city of Jerusalem on it. Then pretend to surround it and attack it. Make some little models of war machines. Build a ramp up to it. Set camps up around it. Surround it with models of logs to be used for knocking down its gates. Then get an iron pan. Put it between you and the city. Pretend it is an iron wall. Turn your face toward the city. It will be under attack when you begin to attack it. That will show the people of Israel what is going to happen to Jerusalem.

A message from the LORD came to me. The LORD said, "Son of man, I am the LORD and King. I say to the land of Israel, 'The end has come! It has come on the four corners of the land. The end has now come for you. I will pour out my anger on you. I will judge you based on how you have lived. I will pay you back for all your evil practices. I hate them.

"I am the LORD and King. I say, 'Horrible trouble is coming! No one has ever heard of anything like it. It is here!

" 'The end has come! The end has come! It has stirred itself up against you. It is here! Death has come on you who live in the land. The time for you to be destroyed has come. The day when it will happen is near. There is no joy on your mountains. There is nothing but panic.

" 'I am about to pour out all my great anger on you. I will judge you based on how you have lived. I will pay you back for all your evil practices. I hate them.

" 'I will not feel sorry for you. I will not spare you. I will pay you back for how you have lived. I will judge you for your evil practices. I hate them. You will know that I am the one who strikes you down. I am the LORD.

" 'Their hands will be powerless to help them. They will wet themselves. They will put on the rough clothing people wear when they're sad. They will put on terror as if it were their clothes. Every face will be covered with shame. Every head will be shaved.

" 'The king will be filled with sadness. The princes will lose all hope. The hands of the people of the land will tremble. I will punish them based on how they have lived. I will judge them by their own standards. Then they will know that I am the LORD.' "

⚬⚬⚬

Then I heard the LORD call out in a loud voice. He said, "Bring here those who are appointed to bring my judgment on the city. Make sure each of them has a weapon in his hand." I saw six men coming from the direction of the upper gate. It faces north. Each of them had a deadly weapon in his hand. A man wearing linen clothes came along with them. He was carrying a writing kit at his side. They came in and stood beside the bronze altar.

The glory of the God of Israel had been above the cherubim. It moved from there to the doorway of the temple. Then the LORD called to the man who was dressed in linen clothes. He had the writing kit. The LORD said to him, "Go all through Jerusalem. Look for those who are sad and sorry about all the things being done there. I hate those things. Put a mark on the foreheads of those people."

I heard him speak to the six men. He said, "Follow him through the city. Do not show any pity or concern. Kill the old men and women, the young men and women, and the children. But do not touch anyone who has the mark. Start at my temple." So they began with the old men who were in front of the temple.

Then he said to the men, "Make the temple 'unclean.' Fill the courtyards with dead bodies. Go!" So they went out and started killing people all through the city. While they were doing it, I was left alone. I fell with my face toward the ground. I cried out, "Lord and King, are you going to destroy all the Israelites who are still left alive? Will you pour out your great anger on all those who remain in Jerusalem?"

He answered me, "The sin of Israel and Judah is very great. The land is full of murderers. Its people are not being fair to one another anywhere in Jerusalem. They say, 'The Lord has deserted the land. He doesn't see us.' So I will not spare them or feel sorry for them. Anything that happens to them will be their own fault."

Then the man wearing linen clothes returned. He had the writing kit. He reported, "I've done what you commanded."

Then the Spirit of the Lord lifted me up. He brought me to the east gate of the Lord's house. There were 25 men at the entrance of the gate. I saw Jaazaniah and Pelatiah among them. They were leaders of the people. Jaazaniah is the son of Azzur. Pelatiah is the son of Benaiah. The Lord said to me, "Son of man, these men are making evil plans. They are giving bad advice to the city. They say, 'Haven't our houses just been built again? The city is like a pot used for cooking. And we are the meat in it.' So prophesy against them. Prophesy, son of man."

Then the Spirit of the Lord came on me. He told me to tell them, "The Lord says, 'You leaders in Israel, that is what you are saying. But I know what you are thinking. You have killed many people in this city. In fact, you have filled its streets with dead bodies.'

"So the Lord and King says, 'The bodies you have thrown there are the meat. And the city is the cooking pot. But I will drive you out of it. You are afraid of the swords of war. But I will bring them against you,' announces the Lord and King. 'I will drive you out of the city. I will hand you over to outsiders. And I will punish you. You will be killed by swords. I will judge you at the borders of Israel. Then you will know that I am the Lord.' "

Pelatiah, the son of Benaiah, died as I was prophesying. Then

I fell with my face toward the ground. I cried out in a loud voice. I said, "LORD and King, will you destroy all the Israelites who are still left alive?"

A message from the LORD came to me. The LORD said, "Son of man, the people of Jerusalem have spoken about you. They have spoken about the others the Babylonians have taken away. They have also spoken about all the other people of Israel. The people of Jerusalem have said, 'Those people are far away from the LORD. This land was given to us. And it belongs to us.'

"So tell them, 'The LORD and King says, "I sent some of my people far away among the nations. I scattered them among the countries. But for a little while I have been their temple in the countries where they have gone." '

"Tell them, 'The LORD and King says, "I will gather you from the nations. I will bring you back from the countries where you have been scattered. I will give you back the land of Israel." '

"They will return to it. They will remove all its statues of evil gods. I hate those gods. I will give my people hearts that are completely committed to me. I will give them a new spirit that is faithful to me. I will remove their stubborn hearts from them. And I will give them hearts that obey me. Then they will follow my rules. They will be careful to keep my laws. They will be my people. And I will be their God. But some people have hearts that are committed to worshiping the statues of their evil gods. I hate those gods. Anything that happens to those people will be their own fault," announces the LORD and King.

Then the cherubim spread their wings. The wheels were beside them. The glory of the God of Israel was above them. The glory of the LORD went up from the city. It stopped above the Mount of Olives east of the city. The Spirit of God lifted me up. He took me to those who had been brought to Babylon as prisoners. These are the things that happened in the visions the Spirit gave me.

Then the visions I had seen were gone. I told my people everything the LORD had shown me.

remember what you read

1. What is something you noticed for the first time?

_____

_____

_____

_____

2. What questions did you have?

_____

_____

_____

_____

3. Was there anything that bothered you?

_____

_____

_____

_____

4. What did you learn about loving God?

_____

_____

_____

_____

5. What did you learn about loving others?

_____

_____

_____

_____

introduction to Ezekiel, part 3

In today's reading, Ezekiel continues to tell stories to the people by his actions. God warns the people about prophets who tell lies. God tells Ezekiel that people are responsible for their own actions. A parent cannot save their child from judgment. God promises to make a new covenant agreement with his people.

⌇⌇⌇

A message from the LORD came to me. The LORD said, "Son of man, you are living among people who refuse to obey me. They have eyes that can see. But they do not really see. They have ears that can hear. But they do not really hear. They refuse to obey me.

"Son of man, pack your belongings as if you were going on a long trip. Leave in the daytime. Let the people see you. Start out from where you are. Go to another place. Perhaps they will understand the meaning of what you are doing. But they will still refuse to obey me. Bring out your belongings packed for a long trip. Do this during the daytime. Let the people see you. Then in the evening, pretend you are being forced to leave home. Let the people see you. While the people are watching, dig through the mud bricks of your house. Then take your belongings out through the hole in the wall. Put them on your shoulder. Carry them out at sunset. Let the people see you. Cover your face so you can't see the land. All of that will show the Israelites what is going to happen to them."

So I did just as he commanded me. During the day I brought out my things as if I were going on a long trip. In the evening I dug through the wall of my house with my hands. At sunset I took my belongings out. I put them on my shoulders. The people watched what I was doing.

In the morning a message from the LORD came to me. The LORD said, "Son of man, didn't the Israelites ask you, 'What are you doing?' They always refuse to obey me.

"Tell them, 'The LORD and King says, "This prophecy is about Zedekiah, the prince in Jerusalem. It is also about all the Israelites who still live there."' Tell them, 'The things I've done are a picture of what's going to happen to you.

"'So what I've done will happen to you. You will be forced to leave home. You will be taken to Babylon as prisoners.'

⟋⟋⟋

A message from the LORD came to me. The LORD said, "Son of man, tremble with fear as you eat your food. Tremble as you drink your water. Speak to the people of the land. Say to them, 'Here is what the LORD and King says. He says this about those who live in Jerusalem and Israel. "They will be worried as they eat their food. They will not have any hope as they drink their water. Their land will be stripped of everything in it because all those who live there are harming one another. The towns where people live will be completely destroyed. The land will become a dry and empty desert. Then you will know that I am the LORD."'"

⟋⟋⟋

A message from the LORD came to me. The LORD said, "Son of man, prophesy against those who are now prophesying in Israel. What they prophesy comes out of their own minds. Tell them, 'Listen to the LORD's message! The LORD and King says, "How terrible it will be for you foolish prophets! You say what your own minds tell you to. Your visions do not come from me. Israel, your prophets are like wild dogs that live among broken-down buildings. You have not repaired the cracks in the city wall for the people of Israel. So it will not stand firm in the battle on the day I judge you. The visions of those prophets are false. They use magic to try to find out what is going to happen. But their magic tricks are lies. They say, 'The Lord announces.' But I have not sent them. In spite of that, they expect him to make their words come true. You prophets have seen false visions. You have used magic to try to find out what is going to happen. But your magic tricks are lies. So you lied when you said, 'The Lord announces.' I did not even speak to you at all."

" 'The Lord and King says, "I am against you prophets. Your messages are false. Your visions do not come true," announces the Lord and King. "Israel, my power will be against the prophets who see false visions. Their magic tricks are lies. They will not be among the leaders of my people. They will not be listed in the records of Israel. In fact, they will not even enter the land. Then you will know that I am the Lord and King.

" ' "They lead my people away from me. They say, 'Peace.' But there isn't any peace. They are like people who build a weak wall. They try to cover up the weakness by painting the wall white. Tell those who do this that their wall is going to fall. Heavy rains will come. I will send hailstones crashing down. Powerful winds will blow. The wall will fall down. Then people will ask them, 'Now where is the paint you covered it with?' "

" 'So the Lord and King speaks. He says, "When I am very angry, I will send a powerful wind. Hailstones and heavy rains will come. They will fall with great force. I will tear down the wall you prophets painted over. I will knock it down. The only thing left will be its foundation. When it falls, you will be destroyed along with it. Then you will know that I am the Lord. So I will pour out all my great anger on the wall. I will also send it against you prophets who painted it. I will say to you, 'The wall is gone. You who painted it will be gone too. You prophets of Israel prophesied to Jerusalem. You saw visions of peace for its people. But there wasn't any peace,' announces the Lord and King." '

"Son of man, turn your attention to the daughters of your people. What they prophesy comes out of their own minds. So prophesy against them. Tell them, 'Here is what the Lord and King says. "How terrible it will be for you women who sew magic charms to put around your wrists! You make veils of different lengths to put on your heads. You do these things to trap people. You trap my people. But you will also be trapped. You have treated me as if I were not holy. You did it among my very own people. You did it for a few handfuls of barley and scraps of bread. You told lies to my people. They like to listen to lies. You killed those who should have lived. And you spared those who should have died."

"'So the Lord and King says, "I am against your magic charms. You use them to trap people as if they were birds. I will tear them off your arms. I will set free the people you trap like birds. I will tear your veils off your heads. I will save my people from your power. They will no longer be under your control. Then you will know that I am the Lord. I had not made godly people sad. But when you told them lies, you made them lose all hope. You advised sinful people not to turn from their evil ways. You did not want them to save their lives. So you will never see false visions again. You will not use your magic tricks anymore. I will save my people from your power. Then you will know that I am the Lord."'"

⚬⟋⟋⟋⚬

A message from the Lord came to me. The Lord said, "Son of man, suppose the people in a certain country sin against me. And they are not faithful to me. So I reach out my powerful hand against them. I cut off their food supply. I make them very hungry. I kill them and their animals. And suppose Noah, Daniel and Job were in that country. Then these three men could save only themselves by doing what is right," announces the Lord and King.

"Or suppose I send a plague into that land. And I pour out my great anger on it by spilling blood. I kill its people and their animals. And suppose Noah, Daniel and Job were in that land. Then they could not save their own sons or daughters. They could save only themselves by doing what is right. And that is just as sure as I am alive," announces the Lord and King.

The Lord and King says, "It will get much worse. I will punish Jerusalem in four horrible ways. There will be war, hunger, wild animals and plague. They will destroy the people and their animals. But some people will be left alive. Some children will be brought out of the city. They will come to you. You will see how they act and the way they live. And you will be comforted in spite of all the trouble I brought on Jerusalem. You will be comforted when you see how they act and the way they live. Then you will know that I did not do anything there without a reason," announces the LORD and King.

❧

The LORD and King says, "I will punish you in keeping with what you have done. I sealed with a promise the covenant I made with you. You hated that promise. And you broke my covenant. But I will remember my covenant with you. I made it with you when you were young. Now I will make a new covenant with you. It will last forever. Then you will remember how you have lived. You will be ashamed when I give you Samaria and Sodom. Samaria is your older sister. Sodom is your younger one. I will give them and their daughters to you as daughters. That can't happen based on my old covenant with you. So I will make my new covenant with you. Then you will know that I am the LORD. I will pay for all the sins you have committed. Then you will remember what you have done. You will be ashamed of it. Because of your shame, you will never speak against me again," announces the LORD and King.

remember what you read

1. What is something you noticed for the first time?

_____
_____
_____
_____

2. What questions did you have?

_____
_____
_____
_____

3. Was there anything that bothered you?

_____
_____
_____
_____

4. What did you learn about loving God?

_____
_____
_____
_____

5. What did you learn about loving others?

_____
_____
_____
_____

EZEKIEL, PART 4

introduction to Ezekiel, part 4

Ezekiel continues to warn that the choices of God's people will destroy them. But he promises that each person will be punished for their own wrong choices, not those of others.

A message from the LORD came to me. The LORD said, "You people have a proverb about the land of Israel. What do you mean by it? It says,

" 'The parents eat sour grapes.
But the children have a bitter taste in their mouths.'

"You will not use that proverb in Israel anymore," announces the LORD and King. "And that is just as sure as I am alive. Everyone belongs to me. Parents and children alike belong to me. A person will die because of their own sins.

"Suppose there is a godly man
who does what is fair and right.
And he does not eat at the mountain temples.
He does not worship the statues of Israel's gods.
He does not treat anyone badly.
Instead, he always returns things he takes
to make sure loans are paid back.
He does not steal.
Instead, he gives his food to hungry people.
He provides clothes for those who are naked.

He does not charge interest when he lends money to them.
　He does not make money from them.
　He keeps himself from doing what is wrong.
　He judges cases fairly.
He obeys my rules.
　He is faithful in keeping my laws.
He always does what is right.
　You can be sure he will live,"
　announces the LORD and King.

"But suppose he has a mean son who harms other people. The son commits murder. Or he does some other things that are wrong. Suppose he does these things even though his father never did.

"Suppose the son eats at the mountain temples.
He treats poor and needy people badly.
　He steals.
He does not pay back what he owes.
　He worships statues of gods.
He does other things I hate.
　He charges interest when he lends money to poor people.
　　He makes money from them.

Will a man like that live? He will not! He must be put to death. And what happens to him will be his own fault. He did many things I hate.

"But suppose this son has a son of his own. And the son sees all the sins his father commits. He sees them, but he does not do them.

"Suppose he does not eat at the mountain temples.
　And he does not worship the statues of Israel's gods.
He does not treat anyone badly.
　He does not make people give him something
　to prove they will pay back what they owe him.
He does not steal.
　Instead, he gives his food to hungry people.
　He provides clothes for those who are naked.

He keeps himself from committing sins.
He does not charge interest when he lends money to poor
    people.
He does not make money from them.
He keeps my laws and obeys my rules.

He will not die because of his father's sin. You can be sure he will live. But his father will die because of his own sin. He got rich by cheating others. He robbed his relatives. He also did what was wrong among his people.

"But you still ask, 'Is the son guilty along with his father?' No! The son did what was fair and right. He was careful to obey all my rules. So you can be sure he will live. A person will die because of their own sins. A child will not be guilty because of what their parent did. And a parent will not be guilty because of what their child did. The right things a godly person does will be added to their account. The wrong things a sinful person does will be charged against them.

"But suppose a sinful person turns away from all the sins they have committed. And they obey all my rules. They do what is fair and right. Then you can be sure they will live. They will not die. None of the sins they have committed will be held against them. Because of the godly things they have done, they will live. When sinful people die, it does not give me any joy," announces the Lord and King. "But when they turn away from their sins and live, that makes me very happy.

"Suppose a godly person stops doing what is right. And they sin. They do the same evil things a sinful person does. They do things I hate. Then they will not live. I will not remember any of the right things they have done. They have not been faithful to me. They have also committed many other sins. So they are guilty. They will die.

"But you say, 'What the Lord does isn't fair.' Listen to me, you Israelites. What I do is always fair. What you do is not. Suppose a godly person stops doing what is right. And they sin. Then they will die because of it. They will die because of the sin they have committed. But suppose a sinful person turns away from the evil things they have done. And they do what is fair and right. Then they will save their life. They think about all the evil things they have done. And they turn away from them. So you can be sure they will live. They will not die.

"So I will judge you Israelites. I will judge each of you in keeping with what you have done," announces the LORD and King. "Turn away from your sins! Turn away from all the evil things you have done. Then sin will not bring you down. Get rid of all the evil things you have done. Let me give you a new heart and a new spirit. Then you will be faithful to me. Why should you die, people of Israel? When anyone dies, it does not give me any joy," announces the LORD and King. "So turn away from your sins. Then you will live!

"Sing a song of sadness about Israel's princes. Say to Israel,

" 'You were like a mother lion to your princes.
　She lay down among the lions.
　She brought up her cubs.
One of them was Jehoahaz.
　He became a strong lion.
He learned to tear apart what he caught.
　And he became a man-eater.
The nations heard about him.
　They trapped him in their pit.
They put hooks in his face.
　And they led him away to Egypt.

" 'The mother lion looked and waited.
　But all her hope was gone.
So she got another one of her cubs.
　She made him into a strong lion.
He prowled with the lions.
　He became very strong.
He learned to tear apart what he caught.
　And he became a man-eater.
He broke down their forts.
　He completely destroyed their towns.

The land and all those who were in it
  were terrified when he roared.
Then nations came against him.
  They came from all around him.
They spread out their net to catch him.
  He was trapped in their pit.
They used hooks to pull him into a cage.
  They brought him to the king of Babylon.
They put him in prison.
  So his roar was not heard anymore
  on the mountains of Israel.

" 'Israel, you were like a vine in a vineyard.
  It was planted near water.
It had a lot of fruit and many branches.
  There was plenty of water.
Its branches were strong.
  Each was good enough to be made into a ruler's scepter.
The vine grew high
  above all the leaves.
It stood out because it was so tall
  and had so many branches.
But Nebuchadnezzar became angry.
  He pulled it up by its roots.
  He threw it to the ground.
The east wind dried it up.
  Its fruit was stripped off.
Its strong branches dried up.
  And fire destroyed them.
Now it is planted in the Babylonian desert.
  It is in a dry and thirsty land.
One of its main branches was Zedekiah.
  Fire spread from it and burned up its fruit.
None of its branches is good enough
  to be made into a ruler's scepter.'

This is a song of sadness. And that is how it should be used."

A message from the LORD came to me. The LORD said, "Son of man, turn your attention to Jerusalem. Preach against the temple. Prophesy against the land of Israel. Tell them, 'The LORD says, "I am against you. I will pull out my sword. I will remove from you godly people and sinful people alike. Because I am going to remove them, my sword will be ready to use. I will strike down everyone from south to north. Then all people will know that I have pulled out my sword. I will not put it back. I am the LORD."'

"Groan, son of man! Groan in front of your people. Groan with a broken heart and bitter sorrow. They will ask you, 'Why are you groaning?' Then you will say, 'Because of the news that is coming. The hearts of all the people will melt away in fear. Their hands will not be able to help them. Their spirits will grow weak. And they will be so afraid they'll wet themselves.' The news is coming! You can be sure those things will happen," announces the LORD and King.

A message from the LORD came to me. The LORD said, "Son of man, prophesy. Say, 'The Lord says,

" ' "A sword! A sword!
A sharp and shiny sword is coming from Babylon!
It is sharpened to kill people.
It flashes like lightning." ' "

The people say, "Should we take delight in the scepter of the LORD's royal son? The sword looks down on every scepter like this." The LORD says,

"I have told Nebuchadnezzar to shine his sword.
It is in his hand.
It has been sharpened and shined.
It is ready for the killer's hand.
Son of man, cry out and weep.
The sword is against my people.
It is against all the princes of Israel.

It will kill them
 along with the rest of my people.
 So beat your chest in sorrow.

"You can be sure that testing will come. Why does the sword
look down on the scepter? Because even the scepter will not continue to rule," announces the LORD and King.

"Son of man, prophesy.
 Clap your hands.
Let the sword strike twice.
 Let it strike even three times.
It is a sword to kill people.
 It is a sword to kill many people.
 It is closing in on them from every side.
People's hearts will melt away in fear.
 Many will be wounded or killed.
I have prepared the sword to kill people
 at all their city gates.
Look! It strikes like lightning.
 It is in the killer's hand.
Sword, cut to the right.
 Then cut to the left.
 Strike down people everywhere your blade is turned.
I too will clap my hands.
 I won't be so angry anymore.
 I have spoken. I am the LORD."

remember what you read

1. What is something you noticed for the first time?

_____

_____

_____

_____

2. What questions did you have?

_____

_____

_____

_____

3. Was there anything that bothered you?

_____

_____

_____

_____

4. What did you learn about loving God?

_____

_____

_____

_____

5. What did you learn about loving others?

_____

_____

_____

_____

introduction to Ezekiel, part 5

Ezekiel is still in Babylon. He shares even more about how terrible the people of Jerusalem act. And he says God is about to destroy the city.

A message from the LORD came to me. The LORD said,

"Son of man, are you going to judge Jerusalem? Will you judge this city that has so many murderers in it? Then tell its people they have done many evil things. I hate those things. Tell them, 'The LORD and King says, "Your city brings death on itself. You spill blood inside its walls. You make yourselves 'unclean' by making statues of gods. You are guilty of spilling blood. Your statues have made you 'unclean.' You have brought your days to a close. The end of your years has come. So the nations will make fun of you. All the countries will laugh at you. Those who are near you will tell jokes about you. So will those who are far away. Trouble fills the streets of your sinful city.

" ' "The princes of Israel are in your city. All of them use their power to spill blood. They have made fun of fathers and mothers alike. They have crushed outsiders. They have treated badly the children whose fathers have died. They have done the same thing to widows. You have looked down on the holy things that were set apart to me. You have misused my Sabbath days. You have spread lies about others so you can spill someone's blood. You eat at the mountain temples. You commit impure acts. You accept money from people who want special favors. You do this to spill

someone's blood. You charge interest to poor people when you
lend them money. You make money from them. You get rich by
cheating your neighbors. And you have forgotten me," announces
the LORD and King.

"'"I will clap my hands because I am so angry. You got rich by
cheating others. You spilled blood inside the walls of your city.
Will you be brave on the day I deal with you? Will you be strong at
that time? I have spoken. I will do this. I am the LORD. I will scatter
you among the nations. I will send you to other countries. I will
put an end to your 'uncleanness.' You will be 'unclean' in the sight
of the nations. Then you will know that I am the LORD."'"

⌘

A message from the LORD came to me. The LORD said, "Son of
man, the people of Israel have become like scum to me. All of them
are like the copper, tin, iron and lead left inside a furnace. They are
only the scum that is removed from silver." So the LORD and King
says, "People of Israel, all of you have become like scum. So I will
gather you together in Jerusalem. People put silver, copper, iron,
lead and tin into a furnace. They melt it with a blazing fire. In the
same way, I will gather you. I will pour out my burning anger on
you. I will put you inside the city and melt you. I will gather you
together. My burning anger will blaze out at you. And you will be
melted inside Jerusalem. Silver is melted in a furnace. And you will
be melted inside the city. Then you will know that I have poured
out my burning anger on you. I am the LORD."

⌘

Another message from the LORD came to me. The LORD said,
"Son of man, speak to the land. Tell it, 'You have not been washed
clean with rain. That's because I am angry with you.' Ezekiel, the
princes of the land are like a roaring lion that tears its food apart.
They eat people up. They take treasures and other valuable things.
They cause many women in the land to become widows. Its priests
break my law. They treat things set apart to me as if they were

not holy. They treat holy and common things as if they were the same. They teach that there is no difference between things that are 'clean' and things that are not. They refuse to keep my Sabbath days. So they treat me as if I were not holy. The officials in the land are like wolves that tear their food apart. They spill blood and kill people to get rich. The prophets cover up these acts for them. The visions of these prophets are false. They use magic to try to find out what is going to happen. But their magic tricks are lies. They say, 'The Lord and King says.' But I have not spoken to them. The people of the land get rich by cheating others. They steal. They crush those who are poor and in need. They treat outsiders badly. They refuse to be fair to them.

"I looked for someone among them who would stand up for Jerusalem. I tried to find someone who would pray to me for the land. Then I would not have to destroy it. But I could not find anyone who would pray for it. So I will pour out my anger on its people. I will destroy them because of my great anger against them. And anything that happens to them will be their own fault," announces the Lord and King.

ᘒᘒᘒ

It was the ninth year since King Jehoiachin had been brought to Babylon as a prisoner. On the tenth day of the tenth month, a message from the Lord came to me. The Lord said, "Son of man, write down today's date. The king of Babylon has surrounded Jerusalem and attacked it today. Your people refuse to obey me. So tell them a story. Say to them, 'The Lord and King told me,

"'"Put a cooking pot on the fire.
    Pour water into it.
Put pieces of meat in it.
    Use all the best pieces.
Use the leg and shoulder.
    Fill it with the best bones.
Pick the finest animal in the flock.
    Pile wood under the pot to cook the bones.

Bring the water to a boil.
    Cook the bones in it." ' "

The Lord and King says,

"How terrible it will be for this city!
    It has so many murderers in it.
How terrible for the pot that is coated with scum!
    The scum on it will not go away.
Take the meat out of the pot piece by piece.
    Take it out in whatever order it comes.

"The blood Jerusalem's people spilled is inside
        its walls.
    They poured it out on a bare rock.
They did not pour it on the ground.
    If they had, dust would have covered it up.
So I put their blood on the bare rock.
    I did not want it to be covered up.
I poured out my great anger on them.
    I paid them back."

So the Lord and King said to me,

"How terrible it will be for this city!
    It has so many murderers in it.
    I too will pile the wood high.
So pile on the wood.
    Light the fire.
Cook the meat well.
    Mix in the spices.
    Let the bones be blackened.
Then set the empty pot on the coals.
    Let it get hot. Let its copper glow.
Then what is not pure in it will melt.
    Its scum will be burned away.
But it can't be cleaned up.
    Its thick scum has not been removed.
    Even fire can't burn it off.

"Jerusalem, you are really impure. I tried to clean you up. But you would not let me make you pure. So you will not be clean again until I am no longer so angry with you.

"I have spoken. The time has come for me to act. I will not hold back. I will not feel sorry for you. I will do what I said I would do. You will be judged for your conduct and actions. I am the LORD," announces the LORD and King.

～～～

A message from the LORD came to me. The LORD said, "Son of man, I will take away from you the wife you delight in. It will happen very soon. But do not sing songs of sadness. Do not let any tears flow from your eyes. Groan quietly. Do not mourn for your wife when she dies. Keep your turban on your head. Keep your sandals on your feet. Do not cover your mustache and beard. Do not eat the food people eat to comfort them when someone dies."

So I spoke to my people in the morning. And in the evening my wife died. The next morning I did what I had been commanded to do.

Then the people said to me, "Tell us what these things have to do with us. Why are you acting like this?"

So I told them. I said, "A message from the LORD came to me. The LORD said, 'Speak to the people of Israel. Tell them, "The LORD and King says, 'I am about to make my temple "unclean." I will let the Babylonians burn it down. It is the beautiful building you are so proud of. You take delight in it. You love it. The sons and daughters you left behind will be killed by swords. So do what Ezekiel did. Do not cover your mustache and beard. Do not eat the food people eat to comfort them when someone dies. Keep your turbans on your heads. Keep your sandals on your feet. Do not mourn or weep. You will waste away because you have sinned so much. You will groan among yourselves. What Ezekiel has done will show you what is going to happen to you. You will do just as he has done. Then you will know that I am the LORD and King.'"'"

"Son of man, I will take away their beautiful temple. It is their joy and glory. They take delight in it. Their hearts long for it. I will also take away their sons and daughters. On the day I destroy everything, a man will escape. He will come and tell you the news. At that time I will open your mouth. Then you will no longer be silent. You will speak with the man. That will show them what will happen to them. And they will know that I am the Lord."

remember what you read

1. What is something you noticed for the first time?

_____

_____

_____

_____

2. What questions did you have?

_____

_____

_____

_____

3. Was there anything that bothered you?

_____

_____

_____

_____

4. What did you learn about loving God?

_____

_____

_____

_____

5. What did you learn about loving others?

_____

_____

_____

_____

introduction to Ezekiel, part 6

Ezekiel started talking about the nations around Israel. God was very upset with several nations. He focused especially on Tyre, a city north of Israel that was home to sailors and merchants, people who bought and sold things that people wanted. They became very rich and proud.

∾℘℘∿

A message from the LORD came to me. The LORD said, "Son of man, turn your attention to the Ammonites. Prophesy against them. Tell them, 'Listen to the message of the LORD and King. He says, "You laughed when my temple was made 'unclean.' You also laughed when the land of Israel was completely destroyed. You mocked the people of Judah when they were taken away as prisoners. So I am going to hand you over to the people of the east. They will set up their tents in your land. They will camp among you. They will eat your fruit. They will drink your milk. I will turn the city of Rabbah into grasslands for camels. Ammon will become a resting place for sheep. Then you will know that I am the LORD." ' " The LORD and King says, "You clapped your hands. You stamped your feet. Deep down inside, you hated the land of Israel. You were glad because of what happened to it. So I will reach out my powerful hand against you. I will give you and everything you have to the nations. I will bring you to an end among the nations. I will destroy you. Then you will know that I am the LORD."

The LORD and King says, "Moab and Edom said, 'Look! Judah has become like all the other nations.' So I will let Moab's enemies attack its lower hills. They will begin at the border towns. Those towns include Beth Jeshimoth, Baal Meon and Kiriathaim. They are the glory of that land. I will hand Moab over to the people of the east. I will also give the Ammonites to them. And the Ammonites will no longer be remembered among the nations. I will punish Moab. Then they will know that I am the Lord."

The Lord and King says, "Edom got even with Judah. That made Edom very guilty." The Lord continues, "I will reach out my hand against Edom. I will kill its people and their animals. I will completely destroy it. They will be killed by swords from Teman all the way to Dedan. I will use my people Israel to pay Edom back. They will punish Edom because my anger against it is great. They will know how I pay back my enemies," announces the Lord and King.

The Lord and King says, "Deep down inside them, the Philistines hated Judah. So the Philistines tried to get even with them. They had been Judah's enemies for many years. So they tried to destroy them." The Lord continues, "I am about to reach out my hand against the Philistines. I will wipe out the Kerethites. I will destroy those who remain along the coast. You can be sure that I will pay them back. I will punish them because my anger against them is great. When I pay them back, they will know that I am the Lord."

～⁓⁓～

It was the first day of the 11th month. It was the 12th year since King Jehoiachin had been brought to Babylon as a prisoner. A message from the Lord came to me. The Lord said, "Son of man, Tyre laughed because of what happened to Jerusalem. The people of Tyre said, 'Jerusalem is the gateway to the nations. But the gate is broken. Its doors have swung open to us. Jerusalem has been destroyed. So now we will succeed.'" The Lord and King says, "But I am against you, Tyre. I will bring many nations against you. They will come in like the waves of the sea. They will destroy your walls. They will pull down your towers. I will clear away the stones of your broken-down buildings. I will turn you into nothing but a bare rock. Out in the Mediterranean Sea your island city will become a place to spread fishnets. I have spoken," announces the Lord and King. "The nations will take you and everything you have. Your settlements on the coast will be destroyed by war. Then you will know that I am the Lord."

The Lord and King speaks to Tyre.

> " 'Famous city, you have been completely destroyed!
>   You were filled with sea traders.
> You and your citizens
>   were a mighty power on the seas.
> You terrified everyone
>   who lived in you.
> The lands along the coast trembled with fear
>   when you fell.
> The islands in the sea
>   were terrified when you were destroyed.' "

The Lord and King says to Tyre, "I will turn you into an empty city. You will be like cities where no one lives anymore. I will cause the ocean to sweep over you. Its mighty waters will cover you. So I will bring you down together with those who go down into the grave. The people there lived long ago. You will have to live in the earth below. It will be like living in buildings that were destroyed many years ago. You will go down into the grave along with others. And you will never come back. You will not take your place in this world again. I will bring you to a horrible end. You will be gone forever. People will look for you. But they will never find you," announces the Lord and King.

⸎

A message from the Lord came to me. The Lord said, "Son of man, sing a song of sadness about Tyre. It is located at the gateway to the Mediterranean Sea. It does business with nations on many coasts. Say to it, 'The Lord and King says,

> " ' "Tyre, you say,
>   'I am perfect and beautiful.'
> You were like a ship that ruled over the high seas.
>   Your builders made you perfect and beautiful.

They cut all your lumber
  from juniper trees on Mount Hermon.
They used a cedar tree from Lebanon
  to make a mast for you.
They made your oars
  out of oak trees from Bashan.
They made your deck out of cypress wood
  from the coasts of Cyprus.
  They decorated it with ivory.
Your sail was made out of beautiful Egyptian linen.
  It served as your banner.
Your shades were made out of blue and purple cloth.
  They were from the coasts of Elishah.
Men from Sidon and Arvad manned your oars.
  Tyre, your sailors were skillful.
Very skilled workers from Byblos were on board.
  They kept you waterproof.
All the ships on the sea and their sailors
  came up beside you.
  They brought their goods to trade for yours.

" ' "Men from Persia, Lydia and Put
  served as soldiers in your army, city of Tyre.
They hung their shields and helmets on your walls.
  That brought glory to you.
Men from Arvad and Helek
  guarded your walls on every side.
Men from Gammad
  were in your towers.
They hung their shields around your walls.
  They made you perfect and beautiful.

꩜

A message from the LORD came to me. The LORD said, "Son of man, speak to Ethbaal. He is the ruler of Tyre. Tell him, 'The LORD and King says,

" ' "In your proud heart
you say, 'I am a god.
I sit on the throne of a god
in the Mediterranean Sea.'
But you are only a human being. You are not a god.
In spite of that, you think you are as wise as a god.
Are you wiser than Daniel?
Isn't even one secret hidden from you?
You are wise and understanding.
So you have become very wealthy.
You have piled up gold and silver
among your treasures.
You have used your great skill in trading
to increase your wealth.
You are very rich.
So your heart has become proud." ' "

The Lord and King says,

"You think you are wise.
In fact, you claim to be as wise as a god.
So I am going to bring outsiders against you.
They will not show you any pity at all.
They will use their swords against your beauty and
wisdom.
They will strike down your shining glory.
They will bring you down to the grave.
You will die a horrible death
in the middle of the sea.
Then will you say, 'I am a god'?
Will you say that to those who kill you?
You will be only a human being to those who kill you.
You will not be a god to them.
You will die just like those who have not been circumcised.
Outsiders will kill you.

I have spoken," announces the Lord and King.

A message from the LORD came to me. The LORD said, "Son of man, sing a song of sadness about the king of Tyre. Tell him, 'The LORD and King says,

" ' "You were the model of perfection.
    You were full of wisdom.
    You were perfect and beautiful.
You were in Eden.
    It was my garden.
All kinds of jewels decorated you.
Here is a list of them.
    carnelian, chrysolite and emerald
    topaz, onyx and jasper
    lapis lazuli, turquoise and beryl
Your settings and mountings were made out of gold.
    On the day you were created,
    they were prepared.
I appointed you to be like a guardian angel.
    I anointed you for that purpose.
You were on my holy mountain.
    You walked among the gleaming jewels.
Your conduct was without blame
    from the day you were created.
    But soon you began to sin.
You traded with many nations.
    You harmed people everywhere.
    And you sinned.
So I sent you away from my mountain in shame.
    Guardian angel, I drove you away
    from among the gleaming jewels.
You thought you were so handsome
    that it made your heart proud.
You thought you were so glorious
    that it spoiled your wisdom.
So I threw you down to the earth.
    I made an example out of you in front of kings.
Your many sins and dishonest trade
    made your holy places impure.

So I made you go up in flames.
  I turned you into nothing but ashes on the ground.
  I let everyone see it.
All the nations that knew you
  are shocked because of what happened to you.
You have come to a horrible end.
  And you will be gone forever." ' "

ⴱⴱⴱ

A message from the Lord came to me. The Lord said, "Son of man, turn your attention to the city of Sidon. Prophesy against it. Say, 'The Lord and King says,

" ' "Sidon, I am against your people.
  Among you I will display my glory.
I will punish your people.
  Among you I will prove that I am holy.
  Then you will know that I am the Lord.
I will send a plague on you.
  I will make blood flow in your streets.
Those who are killed will fall inside you.
  Swords will strike your people on every side.
  Then they will know that I am the Lord.

" ' "The people of Israel will no longer have neighbors who hate them. Those neighbors will not be like sharp and painful thorns anymore. Then Israel will know that I am the Lord and King." ' "

The Lord and King says, "I will gather the people of Israel together from the nations where they have been scattered. That will prove that I am holy. I will let the nations see it. Then Israel will live in their own land. I gave it to my servant Jacob. My people will live there in safety. They will build houses. They will plant vineyards. They will live in safety. I will punish all their neighbors who told lies about them. Then Israel will know that I am the Lord their God."

remember what you read

1. What is something you noticed for the first time?

_____

_____

_____

_____

2. What questions did you have?

_____

_____

_____

_____

3. Was there anything that bothered you?

_____

_____

_____

_____

4. What did you learn about loving God?

_____

_____

_____

_____

5. What did you learn about loving others?

_____

_____

_____

_____

introduction to Ezekiel, part 7

*Ezekiel continues to tell about God's judgment against the nations.
In today's reading, he speaks against Egypt.*

༄༅

It was the tenth year since King Jehoiachin had been brought to
Babylon as a prisoner. On the 12th day of the tenth month, a message from the LORD came to me. The LORD said, "Son of man, turn
your attention to Pharaoh Hophra. He is king of Egypt. Prophesy
against him and the whole land of Egypt. Tell him, 'The LORD and
King says,

" ' "Pharaoh Hophra, I am against you.
    King of Egypt, you are like a huge monster
    lying among your streams.
You say, 'The Nile River belongs to me.
    I made it for myself.'
But I will put hooks in your jaws.
    I will make the fish in your streams
    stick to your scales.
I will pull you out from among your streams.
    All the fish will stick to your scales.
I will leave you out in the desert.
    All the fish in your streams
    will be there with you.
You will fall down in an open field.
    You will not be picked up.

I will feed you to the wild animals
and to the birds in the sky.

Then everyone who lives in Egypt will know that I am the LORD.

" ' "You have been like a walking stick made out of a papyrus stem. The people of Israel tried to lean on you. They took hold of you. But you broke under their weight. You tore open their shoulders. The people of Israel leaned on you. But you snapped in two. And their backs were broken." ' "

So the LORD and King says, "I will send Nebuchadnezzar's sword against you. He will kill people and animals alike. Egypt will become a dry and empty desert. Then your people will know that I am the LORD.

But here is what the LORD and King says. "At the end of 40 years I will gather the Egyptians together. I will bring them back from the nations where they were scattered. I will bring them back from where they were taken as prisoners. I will return them to Upper Egypt. That is where their families came from. There they will be an unimportant kingdom. Egypt will be the least important kingdom of all. It will never place itself above the other nations again. I will make it very weak. Then it will never again rule over the nations. The people of Israel will no longer trust in Egypt. Instead, Egypt will remind them of how they sinned when they turned to it for help. Then they will know that I am the LORD and King."

⌒⌒⌒

A message from the LORD came to me. The LORD said, "Son of man, prophesy. Say, 'The LORD and King says,

" ' "Cry out,
   'A terrible day is coming!'
The day is near.
   The day of the LORD is coming.
It will be a cloudy day.
   The nations have been sentenced to die.

I will send Nebuchadnezzar's sword against Egypt.
   Cush will suffer terribly.
Many will die in Egypt.
   Then its wealth will be carried away.
   Its foundations will be torn down.

The people of Cush, Libya, Lydia, Kub and the whole land of Arabia will be killed by swords. So will the Jews who live in Egypt. They went there from the covenant land of Israel. And the Egyptians will die too." ' "

   It was the 11th year since King Jehoiachin had been brought to Babylon as a prisoner. On the first day of the third month, a message from the LORD came to me. The LORD said, "Son of man, speak to Pharaoh Hophra, the king of Egypt. Also speak to his huge army. Tell him,

" 'Who can be compared with your majesty?
   Think about what happened to Assyria.
   Once it was like a cedar tree in Lebanon.
It had beautiful branches
   that provided shade for the forest.
It grew very high.
   Its top was above all the leaves.
The waters fed it.
   Deep springs made it grow tall.
Their streams flowed
   all around its base.
They made their way
   to all the trees in the fields.
So it grew higher
   than any other tree in the fields.
It grew more limbs.
   Its branches grew long.
   They spread because they had plenty of water.
All the birds in the sky
   made their nests in its limbs.

All the wild animals
  had their babies under its branches.
All the great nations
  lived in its shade.
Its spreading branches
  made it majestic and beautiful.
Its roots went down deep
  to where there was plenty of water.
The cedar trees in my garden
  were no match for it.
The juniper trees
  could not equal its limbs.
The plane trees
  could not compare with its branches.
No tree in my garden
  could match its beauty.
I gave it many branches.
  They made it beautiful.
All the trees in my Garden of Eden
  were jealous of it.' "

So the Lord and King says, "The great cedar tree grew very high. Its top was above all the leaves. It was proud of how tall it was. So I handed it over to the Babylonian ruler of the nations. I wanted him to punish it because it was so evil. I decided to get rid of it. The Babylonians cut it down and left it there. They did not show it any pity at all. Some of its branches fell on the mountains. Others fell in all the valleys. The branches lay broken in all the stream beds in the land. All the nations on earth came out from under its shade. And they went on their way. All the birds settled on the fallen tree. All the wild animals lived among its branches. So trees that receive plenty of water must never grow so high that it makes them proud. Their tops must never be above the rest of the leaves. No other trees that receive a lot of water must ever grow that high. They are appointed to die and go down into the earth below. They will join human beings, who go down to the place of the dead."

The Lord and King says, "Assyria was like a cedar tree. But I brought it down to the place of the dead. On that day I dried up the deep springs of water and covered them. I held its streams back. I shut off its rich supply of water. Because of that, Lebanon was dressed in gloom as if it were clothes. All the trees in the fields dried up. I brought the cedar tree down to the place of the dead. It joined the other nations that go down there. I made the nations on earth shake because of the sound of its fall. Then all the trees of Eden were comforted in the earth below. That included the finest and best trees in Lebanon. And it included all the trees that received plenty of water. Others also went down along with the cedar tree into the place of the dead. They included those who had been killed by swords. They also included the armed men among the nations who lived in its shade.

"Which one of the trees of Eden can be compared with you? What tree is as glorious and majestic as you are? But you too will be brought down to the earth below. There you will join the trees of Eden. You will be among those who were killed by swords.

"That is what will happen to Pharaoh and his huge armies," announces the Lord and King.

⌒⌒⌒

It was the 12th year since King Jehoiachin had been brought to Babylon as a prisoner. On the first day of the 12th month, a message from the Lord came to me. The Lord said, "Son of man, sing a song of sadness about Pharaoh Hophra, the king of Egypt. Tell him,

" 'You are like a lion among the nations.
    You are like a monster in the sea.
You move around wildly in your rivers.
    You churn the water with your feet.
    You make the streams muddy.' "

The Lord and King says,

"I will use a large crowd of people
    to throw my net over you
    They will pull you up in it.

Then I will throw you on the land.
> I will toss you into an open field.
I will let all the birds in the sky settle on you.
> I will let all the wild animals eat you up.
I will scatter the parts of your body all over the mountains.
> I will fill the valleys with your remains.
I will soak the land with your blood.
> It will flow all the way to the mountains.
> The valleys will be filled with the parts of your body.
When I wipe you out,
> I will put a cover over the heavens.
> I will darken the stars.
I will cover the sun with a cloud.
> The moon will stop shining.
I will darken all the bright lights
> in the sky above you.
I will bring darkness over your land,"
> announces the Lord and King.
"The hearts of many people will be troubled.
> That is because I will destroy you among the nations.
> You had never known anything about those lands before.
Many nations will be shocked
> when they see what has happened to you.
Their kings will tremble with fear
> when they find out about it.
I will get ready to use Nebuchadnezzar
> as my sword against them.
On the day you fall from power,
> each of the kings will tremble with fear.
> Each will be afraid he is the next to die."

The Lord and King says,

"I will send against you
> the sword of the king of Babylon.
I will destroy your huge army.
> They will be killed by the swords
> of Babylon's mighty soldiers.

The soldiers will not show them any pity.
  They will bring Egypt down in all its pride.
  Its huge armies will be thrown down.
I will destroy all its cattle
  from the places where they have plenty of water.
Human feet will never stir up the water again.
  The hooves of cattle will not make it muddy anymore.
I will let the waters of Egypt settle.
  I will make its streams flow like olive oil,"
  announces the Lord and King.
"I will turn Egypt into an empty land.
  I will strip away everything in it.
I will strike down everyone who lives there.
  Then they will know that I am the Lord.

"That is the song of sadness people will sing about Egypt. Women from other nations will sing it. They will weep over Egypt and its huge armies," announces the Lord and King.

remember what you read

1. What is something you noticed for the first time?

_____

_____

_____

_____

2. What questions did you have?

_____

_____

_____

_____

3. Was there anything that bothered you?

_____

_____

_____

_____

4. What did you learn about loving God?

_____

_____

_____

_____

5. What did you learn about loving others?

_____

_____

_____

_____

EZEKIEL, PART 8

introduction to Ezekiel, part 8

Now in this last big section, Ezekiel speaks hopeful words for Israel, which is what he calls the people taken from Judah to Babylon. He shares a dramatic vision that God showed him. He saw bones coming to life. This seemed about as likely as God's people returning to Jerusalem. But that was exactly God's promise. God also promised to give his people "new hearts" and a "new spirit that is faithful" to God.

❧

"Son of man, speak to the Israelites. Tell them, 'You are saying, "Our sins and the wrong things we have done weigh us down. We are wasting away because we have sinned so much. So how can we live?"' Tell them, 'When sinful people die, it does not give me any joy. But when they turn away from their sins and live, that makes me very happy. And that is just as sure as I am alive,' announces the LORD and King. 'So turn away from your sins! Change your evil ways! Why should you die, people of Israel?'

❧

It was the 12th year since we had been brought to Babylon as prisoners. On the fifth day of the tenth month, a man who had escaped from Jerusalem came to bring me a report. He said, "The city has fallen!" The evening before the man arrived, the power of the LORD came on me. He opened my mouth before the man came to me in the morning. So my mouth was opened. I was no longer silent.

Then a message from the LORD came to me. The LORD said, "Son of man, here is what the people living in Israel's broken-down buildings are saying. 'Abraham was only one man. But he owned the land. We are many people. The land must certainly belong to us.' So tell them, 'The LORD and King says, "You eat meat that still has blood in it. You worship your statues of gods. You commit murder. So should you still possess the land? You depend on your swords. You do things I hate. So should you still possess the land?"'

"Son of man, your people are talking about you. They are getting together by the walls of their houses and at their doors. They are saying to one another, 'Come. Listen to the LORD's message.' My people come to you, just as they usually do. They sit in front of you. They hear what you say. But they do not put it into practice. With their mouths they say they love me. But in their hearts they want what belongs to others. They try to get rich by cheating them. You are nothing more to them than someone who sings love songs. They say you have a beautiful voice. They think you play an instrument well."

A message from the LORD came to me. The LORD said, "Son of man, prophesy against the shepherds of Israel. Tell them, 'The LORD and King says, "How terrible it will be for you shepherds of Israel! You only take care of yourselves. You should take good care of your flocks. Instead, you eat the butter. You dress yourselves with the wool. You kill the finest animals. But you do not take care of your flocks. You have not made the weak ones in the flock stronger. You have not healed the sick. You have not bandaged those who are hurt. You have not brought back those who have wandered away. You have not searched for the lost. When you ruled over them, you were mean to them. You treated them badly. So they were scattered because they did not have a shepherd. They became food for all of the wild animals. My sheep wandered all over the mountains and high hills. They were scattered over the whole earth. No one searched for them. No one looked for them."

The LORD and King says, "I myself will search for my sheep. I will look after them. A shepherd looks after his scattered flock when he is with them. I will save them from all the places where they were scattered on a dark and cloudy day. I will bring them out from among the nations. I will bring them into their own land. There they will eat grass on the mountains and in the valleys. And they will eat in all the fields of Israel. I will take care of them in the best grasslands. They will eat grass on the highest mountains of Israel. There they will lie down in the finest grasslands. I myself will take care of my sheep. I will let them lie down in safety," announces the LORD and King. "I will search for the lost. I will bring back those who have wandered away. I will bandage the ones who are hurt. I will make the weak ones stronger. But I will destroy those who are fat and strong. I will take good care of my sheep. I will treat them fairly."

The LORD and King says, "You are my flock. I will judge between one sheep and another. I will judge between rams and goats. You already eat in the best grasslands. Must you also stomp all over the other fields? You already drink clear water. Must you also make the rest of the water muddy with your feet? Must my flock have to eat the grass you have stomped on? Must they drink the water you have made muddy?"

So the LORD and King speaks to them. He says, "I myself will judge between the fat sheep and the skinny sheep. You push the other sheep around with your hips and shoulders. You use your horns to butt all the weak sheep. Finally, you drive them away. But I will save my sheep. They will not be carried off anymore. I will judge between one sheep and another. I will place one shepherd over them. He will belong to the family line of my servant David. He will take good care of them. He will look after them. He will be their shepherd. I am the LORD. I will be their God. And my servant from David's family line will be the prince among them. I have spoken. I am the LORD.

"I will make a covenant with them. It promises to give them peace. I will get rid of the wild animals in the land. Then my sheep can live safely in the desert. They can sleep in the forests. I will make them and the places surrounding my holy mountain of Zion a blessing. I will send down rain at the right time. There will be showers of blessing. The trees will bear their fruit. And the ground will produce its crops. The people will be secure in their land. I will break the chains that hold them. I will save them from the power of those who made them slaves. Then they will know that I am the Lord. The nations will not carry them off anymore. Wild animals will no longer eat them up. They will live in safety. And no one will make them afraid. I will give them a land that is famous for its crops. They will never again be hungry there. The nations will not make fun of them anymore. Then they will know that I am with them. I am the Lord their God. And the Israelites will know that they are my people," announces the Lord and King. "You are my sheep. You belong to my flock. And I am your God," announces the Lord and King.

𝓒𝓳𝓳𝓸

"So tell the Israelites, 'The Lord and King speaks. He says, "People of Israel, I will not take action for your benefit. Instead, I will act for the honor of my holy name. You have treated it as if it were not holy. You did it everywhere you went among the nations. But I will show everyone how holy my great name is. You have treated it as if it were not holy. So I will use you to prove to the nations how holy I am. Then they will know that I am the Lord," announces the Lord and King.

" ' "I will take you out of the nations. I will gather you together from all the countries. I will bring you back into your own land. I will sprinkle pure water on you. Then you will be 'clean.' I will make you completely pure and 'clean.' I will take all the statues of your gods away from you. I will give you new hearts. I will give you a new spirit that is faithful to me. I will remove your stubborn hearts from you. I will give you hearts that obey me. I will put my Spirit in you. I will make you want to obey my rules. I want you to be careful to keep my laws. Then you will live in the land I gave your people of long ago. You will be my people. And I will be your God. I will save you from all your 'uncleanness.' I will give you plenty of grain. You will have more than enough. So you will never be hungry again. I will multiply the fruit on your trees. I will increase the crops in your fields. Then the nations will no longer make fun of you because you are hungry," announces the LORD and King.'"

The LORD and King says, "Once again I will answer Israel's prayer. Here is what I will do for them. I will multiply them as if they were sheep. Large flocks of animals are sacrificed at Jerusalem during the appointed feasts there. In the same way, the destroyed cities will be filled with flocks of people. Then they will know that I am the LORD."

⌇⌇⌇

The power of the LORD came on me. His Spirit brought me away from my home. He put me down in the middle of a valley. It was full of bones. He led me back and forth among them. I saw a huge number of bones in the valley. The bones were very dry. The LORD asked me, "Son of man, can these bones live?"

I said, "LORD and King, you are the only one who knows."

Then he said to me, "Prophesy to these bones. Tell them, 'Dry bones, listen to the LORD's message. The LORD and King speaks to you. He says, "I will put breath in you. Then you will come to life again. I will attach tendons to you. I will put flesh on you. I will cover you with skin. So I will put breath in you. And you will come to life again. Then you will know that I am the LORD."'"

So I prophesied just as the LORD commanded me to. As I was prophesying, I heard a noise. It was a rattling sound. The bones came together. One bone connected itself to another. I saw tendons and flesh appear on them. Skin covered them. But there was no breath in them.

Then the LORD said to me, "Prophesy to the breath. Prophesy, son of man. Tell it, 'The LORD and King says, "Breath, come from all four directions. Go into these people who have been killed. Then they can live."'" So I prophesied just as he commanded me to. And breath entered them. Then they came to life again. They stood up on their feet. They were like a huge army.

Then the Lord said to me, "Son of man, these bones stand for all the people of Israel. The people say, 'Our bones are dried up. We've lost all hope. We are destroyed.' So prophesy. Tell them, 'The Lord and King says, "My people, I am going to open up your graves. I am going to bring you out of them. I will take you back to the land of Israel. So I will open up your graves and bring you out of them. Then you will know that I am the Lord. You are my people. I will put my Spirit in you. And you will live again. I will settle you in your own land. Then you will know that I have spoken. I have done it," announces the Lord.' "

remember what you read

1. What is something you noticed for the first time?

_____

_____

_____

_____

2. What questions did you have?

_____

_____

_____

_____

3. Was there anything that bothered you?

_____

_____

_____

_____

4. What did you learn about loving God?

_____

_____

_____

_____

5. What did you learn about loving others?

_____

_____

_____

_____

EZEKIEL, PART 9

introduction to Ezekiel, part 9

As part of God's work of bringing back his people, he shows Ezekiel plans for building a new temple. The temple was where God met with his people. The people heard about these plans. It gave them courage and hope that God would keep his promises to rebuild their nation.

❀

The LORD and King says, "I will now cause the people of Jacob to recover from my judgment. I will show my tender love for all the people of Israel. I will make sure that my name is kept holy. My people will forget the shameful things they have done. They will not remember all the ways they were unfaithful to me. They used to live in safety in their land. At that time no one made them afraid. So I will bring them back from the nations. I will gather them from the countries of their enemies. And I will use them to prove to many nations how holy I am. Then they will know that I am the LORD their God. I let the nations take my people away as prisoners. But now I will bring them back to their own land. I will not leave anyone behind. I will no longer turn my face away from the people of Israel. I will pour out my Spirit on them," announces the LORD and King.

❀

It was the 14th year after Jerusalem had been captured. We had been brought to Babylon as prisoners. It was the tenth day of a month near the beginning of the 25th year after that. On that day the power of the LORD came on me. He took me back to my land. In visions God gave me, he brought me to the land of Israel. He set me on a very high mountain. Some buildings were on the south side of it. They looked like a city. He took me there. I saw a man who appeared to be made out of bronze. He was standing at the gate of the outer courtyard. He was holding a linen measuring tape and a measuring rod. The man said to me, "Son of man, look carefully and listen closely. Pay attention to everything I show you. That is why the LORD brought you here. Tell the people of Israel everything you see."

I saw a wall that completely surrounded the temple area. The measuring rod in the man's hand was 11 feet long. He measured the wall with it. The wall was as thick and as high as one measuring rod.

A room with a doorway was by the porch of each inner gateway. The burnt offerings were washed there. On each side of the porch of the gateway were two tables. The burnt offerings were killed on them. So were the sin offerings and guilt offerings. Two more tables were by the outer wall of the gateway porch. They were near the steps at the entrance of the north gateway. Two more tables were on the other side of the steps. So there were four tables on each side of the gateway. The total number of tables was eight. Animals for sacrifice were killed on all of them. There were also four other tables for the burnt offerings. They were made out of blocks of stone. Each table was two and a half feet long and two and a half feet wide. And each was almost two feet high. The tools for killing the burnt offerings and other sacrifices were placed on them. Large hooks hung on the walls all around. Each was three inches long. The meat of the offerings was placed on the tables.

Then the man measured the courtyard. It was square. It measured 175 feet long and 175 feet wide. And the altar was in front of the temple.

Then the man brought me to the main hall. There he measured the doorposts. Each of them was 11 feet wide. The entrance was 18 feet wide. Each of its side walls was almost nine feet wide. He also measured the main hall. It was 70 feet long and 35 feet wide.

Then he went into the Most Holy Room. There he measured

the doorposts at the entrance. Each one of them was three and a half feet wide. The entrance itself was 11 feet wide. Each of its side walls was a little over 12 feet wide. He also measured the Most Holy Room. It was 35 feet long and 35 feet wide. He said to me, "This is the Most Holy Room." It was beyond the back wall of the main hall.

Then the man measured the temple. It was 175 feet long. The open area and the large building behind the temple also measured 175 feet. The east side of the inner courtyard was 175 feet wide. That included the front of the temple.

The main hall and the Most Holy Room were covered with wood. And the porch that faced the inner courtyard was covered with wood. So were the gateways, narrow openings and walkways around these three places. The gateways and everything beyond them were covered with wood. The floor, the wall up to the openings, and the openings themselves were also covered. The area above the outside of the entrance to the Most Holy Room was decorated. There were also decorations all around the walls of the Most Holy Room. Carved cherubim and palm trees were used in the decorations. Each cherub had a palm tree next to it. And each palm tree had a cherub next to it. Each cherub had two faces. One was the face of a human being. It looked toward the palm tree on one side. The other was the face of a lion. It looked toward the palm tree on the other side. The decorations were carved all around the whole temple. Cherubim and palm trees decorated the wall of the main hall. They were carved from the floor all the way up to the area above the entrance.

The man finished measuring what was inside the temple area. Then he led me out through the east gate. He measured all around the area. He measured the east side with his measuring rod. It was 875 feet long. He measured the north side. It was 875 feet long. He measured the south side. It was 875 feet long. Finally, he turned and measured the west side. It was 875 feet long. So he measured the area on all four sides. It had a wall around it. The wall was 875 feet long and 875 feet wide. It separated what was holy from what was not.

Then the man brought me to the east gate. There I saw the glory of the God of Israel. He was coming from the east. His voice was like the roar of rushing waters. His glory made the land shine brightly. The vision I saw was like the one I had when he came to destroy the city. It was also like the visions I had seen by the Kebar River. I fell with my face toward the ground. The glory of the Lord entered the temple through the east gate. Then the Spirit lifted me up. He brought me into the inner courtyard. The glory of the Lord filled the temple.

The man was standing beside me. I heard someone speaking to me from inside the temple. He said, "Son of man, this is the place where my throne is. The stool for my feet is also here. I will live here among the people of Israel forever. They will never again treat my name as if it were not holy. They and their kings will not serve other gods anymore. The people will no longer make funeral offerings for their kings. The people of Israel placed their own doorway next to my holy doorway. They put their doorposts right beside mine. Nothing but a thin wall separated us. They treated my name as if it were not holy. I hated it when they did that. So I became angry with them and destroyed them. Now let them stop serving other gods. Let them stop making funeral offerings for their kings. If they obey me, I will live among them forever.

"Son of man, tell the people of Israel about the temple. Then they will be ashamed of their sins. Let them think carefully about how perfect it is. What if they are ashamed of everything they have done? Then show them all the plans of the temple. Explain to them how it is laid out. Tell them about its exits and entrances. Show them exactly what it will look like. Give them all its rules and laws. Write everything down so they can see it. Then they will be faithful to its plan. And they will obey all its rules.

"Here is the law of the temple. The whole area on top of Mount Zion will be very holy. That is the law of the temple."

The man said, "Here is the size of the altar. The standard measurement I am using is 21 inches. The altar has a drain on the ground. The drain is 21 inches deep and 21 inches wide. It has a rim that is nine inches wide around the edge. Here is how high the altar is. From the drain to the lower ledge is three and a half feet. The lower ledge goes around the altar and is 21 inches wide. From the lower ledge to the upper ledge is seven feet. The upper ledge also goes around the altar and is 21 inches wide. The top part of the altar is where the sacrifices are burned. It is seven feet high. A horn sticks out from each of its four corners. The top part of the altar is square. It is 21 feet long and 21 feet wide. The upper ledge is also square. It is 25 feet long and 25 feet wide. The drain goes all the way around the altar. The rim of the drain is 11 inches wide. The steps leading up to the top of the altar face east."

Then the man said to me, "Son of man, the Lord and King speaks. He says, 'Here are the rules for the altar when it is built. Follow them when you sacrifice burnt offerings and splash blood against it. Give a young bull to the priests as a sin offering. They are Levites from the family of Zadok. They approach me to serve me,' announces the Lord and King. 'Get some of the bull's blood. Put it on the four horns of the altar. Also put it on the four corners of the upper ledge of the altar and all around the rim. That will make the altar pure and "clean." Use the bull for the sin offering. Burn it in the proper place outside the temple.

" 'On the second day offer a male goat. It must not have any flaws. It is a sin offering to make the altar pure and "clean." So do the same thing with the goat that you did with the bull. When you finish making the altar pure, offer a young bull and a ram from the flock. They must not have any flaws. Offer them to me. The priests must sprinkle salt on them. Then they must sacrifice them as a burnt offering to me.

" 'Provide a male goat each day for seven days. It is a sin offering. Also provide a young bull and a ram from the flock. They must not have any flaws. For seven days the priests must make the altar pure and "clean." That is how they will set it apart to me. From the eighth day on, the priests must bring your burnt offerings and friendship offerings. They must sacrifice them on the altar. Then I will accept you,' announces the Lord and King."

remember what you read

1. What is something you noticed for the first time?

_____

_____

_____

_____

2. What questions did you have?

_____

_____

_____

_____

3. Was there anything that bothered you?

_____

_____

_____

_____

4. What did you learn about loving God?

_____

_____

_____

_____

5. What did you learn about loving others?

_____

_____

_____

_____

EZEKIEL, PART 10

Introduction to Ezekiel, part 10

Ezekiel ends his book describing how the land and the city will be divided up and given to the people. He gives the rules for how the priests and people should live. And God promises to live with them.

⌒ᲔᲔᲔ⌒

Then the man brought me back to the outer gate of the temple. It was the one that faced east. It was shut. The LORD said to me, "This gate must remain shut. It must not be opened. No one can enter through it. It must remain shut because I have entered through it. I am the God of Israel. The prince is the only one who can sit in the gateway. There he can eat in front of me. He must enter through the porch of the gateway. And he must go out the same way."

Then the man brought me through the north gate. He took me to the front of the temple. I looked up and saw the glory of the LORD. It filled his temple. I fell with my face toward the ground.

The LORD said to me, "Son of man, pay attention. Look carefully. Listen closely to everything I tell you. I'm telling you about all the rules and instructions concerning my temple. Pay attention to the entrance to the temple and to all its exits. Speak to the people of Israel. They refuse to obey me. Tell them, 'Here is what the LORD and King says. "People of Israel, I have had enough of your evil practices. I hate them. No outsider whose heart is stubborn can enter my temple. They have not been circumcised. Even if they live among the people of Israel they can't enter my temple.

"Some Levites wandered far away from me when Israel went astray. They worshiped the statues of their gods. So they will be punished because they have sinned. They might serve in my temple. They might be in charge of its gates. They might kill the burnt offerings and sacrifices for the people. And they might stand in front of the people and serve them in other ways. But these Levites served the people of Israel. They served while the Israelites were worshiping the statues of their gods. They made the people fall into sin. So I raised my hand and made a promise. I warned them that I would punish them because of their sin," announces the LORD and King. "They must not approach me to serve me as priests. They must not come near any of my holy things. They must stay away from my very holy offerings. They did many things they should have been ashamed of. I hated those things. But I will still appoint them to guard the temple. They will guard it for all the work that has to be done there.

"But the priests must approach me to serve me. They are Levites from Zadok's family line. They guarded my temple when the people of Israel turned away from me. These priests must serve me by offering sacrifices of fat and blood," announces the LORD and King. "They are the only ones who can enter my temple. Only they can come near to serve me as guards.

"When people do not agree, the priests must serve as judges between them. They must make their decisions based on my laws. They must obey my laws and rules for all my appointed feasts. And they must keep my Sabbath days holy.

"A priest must not make himself 'unclean' by going near a dead person. But suppose the dead person was his father or mother. Or suppose it was his son or daughter or brother or unmarried sister. Then the priest may make himself 'unclean.' After he is pure and 'clean' again, he must wait seven days. Then he may go to the inner courtyard to serve in the temple. But when he does, he must sacrifice a sin offering for himself," announces the LORD and King.

"The priests will not receive any part of the land of Israel. I myself will be their only share. They will eat the grain offerings, sin offerings and guilt offerings. Everything in Israel that is set apart to me in a special way will belong to them. The best of every first share of the people's crops will belong to the priests. So will all their special gifts. The people must give the priests the first share of their ground meal. Then I will bless my people's families. The priests must not eat any bird or animal that is found dead. They must not eat anything that wild animals have torn apart.

"People of Israel, you will divide up the land you will receive. When you do, give me my share of it. It will be a sacred area. It will be eight miles long and six and a half miles wide. The entire area will be holy. The temple area in it will be 875 feet long and 875 feet wide. An 88-foot strip around it will be open land. In the sacred area, measure off a large strip of land. It will be eight miles long and three and a third miles wide. The temple will be in it. It will be the most holy place of all. The large strip will be the sacred share of land for the priests. There they will serve in the temple. And they will approach me to serve me there. Their houses will be built on that land. The holy temple will also be located there. So the Levites will serve in the temple. They will have an area eight miles long and three and a third miles wide. The towns they live in will be located there.

"Give the city an area one and two-thirds miles wide and eight miles long. It will be right next to the sacred area. It will belong to all the people of Israel.

"The prince will have land on both sides of the sacred area and the city. Its border will run east and west along the land of one of the tribes. The prince will own this land in Israel. And my princes will not crush my people anymore. Instead, they will allow the people of Israel to receive their own share of land. It will be divided up based on their tribes."

The LORD and King says, "Princes of Israel, you have gone far enough! Stop hurting others. Do not crush them. Do what is fair and right. Stop taking my people's land away from them," announces the LORD and King. "Use weights and measures that are honest and exact. Use the same standard to measure dry and liquid products. Use a 6-bushel measure for dry products. And use a 60-gallon measure for liquids. Every amount of money must be weighed out in keeping with the standard weights.

"Keep the Passover Feast on the 14th day of the first month. It will last for seven days. During that time you must eat bread made without yeast. The prince must provide a bull as a sin offering. It will be for him and all the people of the land. For each of the seven days of the feast he must provide seven bulls and seven rams. They must not have any flaws. They will be a burnt offering to me. The prince must also provide a male goat for a sin offering. He must bring 35 pounds for each bull or ram. He must also provide four quarts of olive oil for each of them.

The man brought me back to the entrance to the temple. I saw water flowing east from under a temple gateway. The temple faced east. The water was coming down from under the south side of the temple. It was flowing south of the altar. Then he brought me out through the north gate of the outer courtyard. He led me around the outside to the outer gate that faced east. The water was flowing from the south side of the east gate.

Then he led me back to the bank of the river. When I arrived there, I saw many trees. They were on both sides of the river. The man said to me, "This water flows toward the eastern territory. It goes down into the Arabah Valley. There it enters the Dead Sea. When it empties into it, the salt water there becomes fresh. Many creatures will live where the river flows. It will have many schools of fish. This water flows there and makes the salt water fresh. So where the river flows everything will live. People will stand along the shore to fish. From En Gedi all the way to En Eglaim there will be places for spreading fishnets. The Dead Sea will have many kinds of fish. They will be like the fish in the Mediterranean Sea. But none of the swamps will have fresh water in them. They will stay salty. Fruit trees of all kinds will grow on both banks of the river. Their leaves will not dry up. The trees will always have fruit on them. Every month they will bear fruit. The water from the temple will flow to them. Their fruit will be used for food. And their leaves will be used for healing."

Here is what the LORD and King says. "People of Israel, here are the borders of the land that you will divide up. You will divide up the land among the 12 tribes of Israel. Each tribe will receive a share. But the family of Joseph will have two shares. Divide the land into equal parts. Long ago I raised my hand and made a promise.

I promised to give the land to your people of long ago. So all of it will belong to you.

"You must divide up this land among yourselves. Do this based on the number of men in your tribes. Each of the tribes must receive a share of the land. You must also give some land to the outsiders who live among you and who have children. Treat them as if they had been born in Israel. Let them have some land among your tribes. Outsiders can live in the land of any tribe. There you must give them their share," announces the Lord and King.

"You must give one share as a special gift to me. It will border the territory of Judah from east to west. It will be eight miles wide. It will be as long as the border of each of the territories of the tribes. Its border will run from east to west. The temple will be in the center of that strip of land.

"Give that special share of land to me. It will be eight miles long and three and a third miles wide. It will be the sacred share of land for the priests. It will be eight miles long on the north side. It will be three and a third miles wide on the west side. It will be three and a third miles wide on the east side. And it will be eight miles long on the south side. My temple will be in the center of it. This share of land will be for the priests who are set apart to me. They will come from the family line of Zadok. The members of that family served me faithfully. They did not go astray as the Levites and other Israelites did. Their share of land will be a special gift to them. It will be part of the sacred share of the land. It will be very holy. Its border will run along the territory of the Levites.

"The city will be six miles around.

"From that time on, its name will be 'The Lord Is There.'"

remember what you read

1. What is something you noticed for the first time?

_____

_____

_____

_____

2. What questions did you have?

_____

_____

_____

_____

3. Was there anything that bothered you?

_____

_____

_____

_____

4. What did you learn about loving God?

_____

_____

_____

_____

5. What did you learn about loving others?

_____

_____

_____

_____

HAGGAI; ZECHARIAH, PART 1

Introduction to Haggai

Haggai was in Babylon. He returned to Jerusalem with those going back to the homeland. But the temple was not rebuilt for about 16 years because some mean neighbors stopped the work. Haggai encouraged the people to finish building God's temple, so everyone could live with God's blessing.

༄༅

A message from the LORD came to Haggai the prophet. Haggai gave it to Zerubbabel and Joshua. Zerubbabel was governor of Judah and the son of Shealtiel. Joshua was high priest and the son of Jozadak. The message came on the first day of the sixth month of the second year that Darius was king of Persia. Here is what Haggai said.

Here is what the LORD who rules over all says. "The people of Judah say, 'It's not yet time to rebuild the LORD's temple.'"

So the message from the LORD came to me. The LORD said, "My temple is still destroyed. But you are living in your houses that have beautiful wooden walls."

The LORD who rules over all says, "Think carefully about how you are living. You have planted many seeds. But the crops you have gathered are small. So you eat. But you never have enough. You drink. But you are never full. You put on your clothes. But you are not warm. You earn your pay. But it will not buy everything you need."

He continues, "Think carefully about how you are living. Go

up into the mountains. Bring logs down. Use them to rebuild the temple, my house. Then I will enjoy it. And you will honor me," says the LORD. "You expected a lot. But you can see what a small amount it turned out to be. I blew away what you brought home. I'll tell you why," announces the LORD who rules over all. "Because my temple is still destroyed. In spite of that, each one of you is busy with your own house. So because of what you have done, the heavens have held back the dew. And the earth has not produced its crops. I ordered the rain not to fall on the fields and mountains. Then the ground did not produce any grain. There were not enough grapes to make fresh wine. The trees did not bear enough olives to make oil. People and cattle suffered. All your hard work failed."

⸙

The LORD says, "In a little while I will shake the heavens and the earth once more. I will also shake the ocean and the dry land. I will shake all the nations. Then what is desired by all nations will come to my temple. And I will fill the temple with glory," says the LORD who rules over all. "The silver belongs to me. So does the gold," announces the LORD who rules over all. "The new temple will be more beautiful than the first one was," says the LORD. "And in this place I will bring peace," announces the LORD who rules over all.

⸙

A final message from the LORD came to Haggai. This message also came on the 24th day of the ninth month. The LORD said, "Speak to Zerubbabel, the governor of Judah. Tell him I am going to shake the heavens and the earth. I will throw down royal thrones. I will smash the power of other kingdoms. I will destroy chariots and their drivers. Horses and their riders will fall. They will be killed by the swords of their relatives.

" 'Zerubbabel, at that time I will pick you,' announces the LORD. 'You are my servant,' announces the LORD. 'You will be like a ring that has my royal mark on it. I have chosen you,' announces the LORD who rules over all."

introduction to Zechariah, part 1

Zechariah's message in the first big part of his book is very similar to Haggai's message. He tells the people the time is right to rebuild the temple. But he also warns them about fasting. This was when they stopped eating for a certain amount of time to show they relied only on God. He says if they don't live the way the covenant agreement tells them to with love and according to the law, their fasting is useless.

∾∾∾

A message from the LORD came to Zechariah the prophet. Zechariah was the son of Berekiah. Berekiah was the son of Iddo. It was the eighth month of the second year that Darius was king of Persia. Here is what Zechariah said.

The LORD who rules over all was very angry with your people of long ago. And now he says to us, "Return to me. Then I will return to you," announces the LORD. "Do not be like your people of long ago. The earlier prophets gave them my message. I said, 'Stop doing what is evil. Turn away from your sinful practices.' But they would not listen to me. They would not pay any attention," announces the LORD. "Where are those people now? And what about my prophets? Do they live forever? I commanded my servants the prophets what to say. I told them what I planned to do. But your people refused to obey me. So I had to punish them.

"Then they had a change of heart. They said, 'The LORD who rules over all has punished us because of how we have lived. He was fair and right to do that. He has done to us just what he decided to do.'"

∾∾∾

"Come, people of Zion! Escape, you who live in Babylon!" The LORD rules over all. His angel says to Israel, "The Glorious One has sent me to punish the nations that have robbed you of everything. That's because anyone who hurts you hurts those the LORD loves and guards. So I will raise my powerful hand to strike down your enemies. Their own slaves will rob them of everything. Then you will know that the Lord who rules over all has sent me.

" 'People of Zion, shout and be glad! I am coming to live among you,' announces the Lord. 'At that time many nations will join themselves to me. And they will become my people. I will live among you,' says the Lord. Then you will know that the Lord who rules over all has sent me to you. He will receive Judah as his share in the holy land. And he will choose Jerusalem again. All you people of the world, be still because the Lord is coming. He is getting ready to come down from his holy temple in heaven."

Then the Lord showed me Joshua the high priest. He was standing in front of the angel of the Lord.

Then the angel spoke to Joshua. He said, "The Lord who rules over all says, 'You must obey me. You must do what I have commanded. Then you will rule in my temple. You will be in charge of my courtyards. And I will give you a place among these who are standing here.

"A message from the Lord came to Zerubbabel. The Lord said, 'Your strength will not get my temple rebuilt. Your power will not do it either. Only the power of my Spirit will do it,' says the Lord who rules over all.

"So nothing can stop Zerubbabel from completing the temple. Even a mountain of problems will be smoothed out by him. When the temple is finished, he will put its most important stone in place. Then the people will shout, 'God bless it! God bless it!' "

Then a message from the Lord came to me. His angel said, "The hands of Zerubbabel have laid the foundation of this temple. His hands will also complete it. Then you will know that the Lord who rules over all has sent me to you.

⸙

A message from the Lord came to me. His angel said, "Get some silver and gold from Heldai, Tobijah and Jedaiah. They have just come back from Babylon. On that same day go to Josiah's house. He is the son of Zephaniah. Use the silver and gold to make a crown. Set it on the head of Joshua the high priest. He is the son of Jozadak. Give Joshua a message from the LORD who rules over all. He says, 'Here is the man whose name is the Branch. He will branch out and build my temple. That is what he will do. He will be dressed in majesty as if it were his royal robe. He will sit as king on his throne. He will also be a priest there. So he will combine the positions of king and priest in himself.' The crown will be given to Heldai, Tobijah, Jedaiah and Zephaniah's son Hen. The crown will be kept in the LORD's temple. It will remind everyone that the LORD's promises will come true. Those who are far away will come to Jerusalem. They will help build the LORD's temple. Then his people will know that the LORD who rules over all has sent me to them. It will happen if they are careful to obey the LORD their God."

※

During the fourth year that Darius was king, a message from the LORD came to me. It was the fourth day of the ninth month. That's the month of Kislev. The people of Bethel wanted to ask the LORD for his blessing. So they sent Sharezer and Regem-Melek and their men. They went to the prophets and priests at the LORD's temple. They asked them, "Should we mourn and go without eating in the fifth month? That's what we've done for many years."

Then the message came to me from the LORD who rules over all. He said, "Ask the priests and all the people in the land a question for me. Say to them, 'You mourned and fasted in the fifth and seventh months. You did it for the past 70 years. But did you really do it for me? And when you were eating and drinking, weren't you just enjoying good food for yourselves? Didn't I tell you the same thing through the earlier prophets? That was when Jerusalem and the towns around it were at rest and enjoyed success. People lived in the Negev Desert and the western hills at that time.'"

Another message from the LORD came to me. Here is what the LORD who rules over all said to his people. "Treat everyone with justice. Show mercy and tender concern to one another. Do not take advantage of widows. Do not mistreat children whose fathers have died. Do not be mean to outsiders or poor people. Do not make evil plans against one another."

But they refused to pay attention to the LORD. They were stubborn. They turned their backs and covered their ears. They made their hearts as hard as the hardest stone. They wouldn't listen to the law. They wouldn't pay attention to the LORD's messages. So the LORD who rules over all was very angry. After all, his Spirit had spoken to his people through the earlier prophets.

"When I called, they did not listen," says the LORD. "So when they called, I would not listen. I used a windstorm to scatter them among all the nations. They were strangers there. The land they left behind became dry and empty. No one could even travel through it. This is how they turned the pleasant land into a dry and empty desert."

A message came to me from the LORD who rules over all.

He said, "I am very jealous for my people in Zion. In fact, I am burning with jealousy for them."

He continued, "I will return to Zion. I will live among my people in Jerusalem. Then Jerusalem will be called the Faithful City. And my mountain will be called the Holy Mountain."

He continued, "Once again old men and women will sit in the streets of Jerusalem. All of them will be using canes because they are old. The city streets will be filled with boys and girls. They will be playing there."

He continued, "All of that might seem hard to believe to the people living then. But it will not be too hard for me."

He continued, "I will save my people. I will gather them from the countries of the east and the west. I will bring them back to live in Jerusalem. They will be my people. I will be their faithful God. I will keep my promises to them."

remember what you read

1. What is something you noticed for the first time?

_____

_____

_____

_____

2. What questions did you have?

_____

_____

_____

_____

3. Was there anything that bothered you?

_____

_____

_____

_____

4. What did you learn about loving God?

_____

_____

_____

_____

5. What did you learn about loving others?

_____

_____

_____

_____

ZECHARIAH, PART 2

introduction to Zechariah, part 2

*The last part of Zechariah does not have dates or a prophet's name.
So he may be quoting someone else to remind the people of the
terrible suffering that comes from disobeying God. But the best words
of hope are that God is going to bring people from all nations to
worship him. And he will bring peace that lasts forever.*

This is a prophecy.

A people who come from several nations will take over
    Ashdod.
  The Lord says, "I will put an end to the pride of the
    Philistines.
They will no longer drink the blood of their animal sacrifices.
  I will remove the 'unclean' food from between their teeth.
The Philistines who are left will belong to our God.
  They will become a family group in Judah.
And Ekron will be like the Jebusites.
  So the Philistines will become part of Israel.
But I will camp at my temple.
  I will guard it against enemy armies.
No one will ever crush my people again.
  I will make sure it does not happen.

"City of Zion, be full of joy!
  People of Jerusalem, shout!

See, your king comes to you.
  He always does what is right.
  He has won the victory.
He is humble and riding on a donkey.
  He is sitting on a donkey's colt.
I will take the chariots away from Ephraim.
  I will remove the war horses from Jerusalem.
  I will break the bows that are used in battle.
Your king will announce peace to the nations.
  He will rule from ocean to ocean.
His kingdom will reach from the Euphrates River
  to the ends of the earth.
I will set your prisoners free
  from where their enemies are keeping them.
I will do it because of the blood
  that put into effect my covenant with you.
Return to your place of safety,
  you prisoners who still have hope.
Even now I announce that I will give you back
  much more than you had before.

The LORD who rules over all says,

"I am very angry with the shepherds.
  I will punish the leaders.
The LORD will take care of his flock.
  They are the people of Judah.
  He will make them like a proud horse in battle.
The most important building stone
  will come from the tribe of Judah.
  The tent stake will also come from it.
And the bow that is used in battle will come from it.
  In fact, every ruler will come from it.
Together they will be like warriors in battle.
  They will stomp their enemies
  into the mud of the streets.
The LORD will be with them.
  So they will fight against the horsemen
  and put them to shame.

"I will make the family of Judah strong.
   I will save the tribes of Joseph.
I will bring them back
   because I have tender love for them.
It will be as if
   I had not sent them away.
I am the LORD their God.
   I will help them.
I will make my people strong.
   They will live in safety because of me,"
announces the LORD.

⚬⚬⚬

This is a prophecy. It is the LORD's message about Israel.

The LORD spreads out the heavens. He lays the foundation of the earth. He creates the human spirit within a person. He says, "Jerusalem will be like a cup in my hand. It will make all the surrounding nations drunk from the wine of my anger. Judah will be attacked by its enemies. So will Jerusalem. At that time all the nations on earth will gather together against Jerusalem. Then it will become like a rock that can't be moved. All the nations that try to move it will only hurt themselves. On that day I will fill every horse with panic. I will make every rider crazy," announces the LORD. "I will watch over the people of Judah. But I will make all the horses of the nations blind. Then the family groups of Judah will say in their hearts, 'The people of Jerusalem are strong. That's because the LORD who rules over all is their God.'

"At that time Judah's family groups will be like a fire pot in a pile of wood. They will be like a burning torch among bundles of grain. They will destroy all the surrounding nations on every side. But Jerusalem will remain unharmed in its place.

"I will save the houses in Judah first. The honor of David's family line is great. So is the honor of those who live in Jerusalem. But their honor will not be greater than the honor of the rest of Judah. At that time I will be like a shield to those who live in Jerusalem. Then even the weakest among them will be great warriors like

David. And David's family line will be like the angel of the LORD who leads them. On that day I will begin to destroy all the nations that attack Jerusalem.

"I will pour out a spirit of grace and prayer on David's family line. I will also send it on those who live in Jerusalem. They will look to me. I am the one they have pierced. They will mourn over me as someone mourns over an only child who has died. They will be full of sorrow over me. Their sorrow will be just like someone's sorrow over an oldest son. At that time there will be a lot of weeping in Jerusalem. It will be as great as the weeping of the people at Hadad Rimmon. Hadad Rimmon is in the valley of Megiddo. They were weeping over Josiah's death. Everyone in the land will mourn. Each family will mourn by themselves and their wives by themselves. That will include the family lines of David, Nathan, Levi, Shimei and all the others.

"At that time a fountain will be opened for the benefit of David's family line. It will also bless the others who live in Jerusalem. It will wash away their sins. It will make them pure and 'clean.'

"On that day I will remove the names of other gods from the land. They will not even be remembered anymore," announces the LORD who rules over all. "I will drive the evil prophets out of the land. I will get rid of the spirit that put lies in their mouths. Some people might still prophesy. But their own fathers and mothers will speak to them. They will tell them, 'You must die. You have told lies in the LORD's name.' When they prophesy, their own parents will stab them.

"At that time every prophet will be ashamed of the vision they see. They will no longer pretend to be a true prophet. They will not put on clothes that are made out of hair in order to trick people. In fact, each one will say, 'I'm not really a prophet. I'm a farmer. I've farmed the land since I was young.' Suppose someone asks, 'What are these wounds on your body?' Then they will answer, 'I was given these wounds at the house of my friends.'

The day of the LORD is coming, Jerusalem. At that time your enemies will steal everything your people own. They will divide it up within your walls.

The LORD will gather all the nations together. They will fight against Jerusalem. They'll capture the city. Its houses will be robbed. Half of the people will be taken away as prisoners. But the rest of them won't be taken. Then the LORD will march out and fight against those nations. He will fight as on a day of battle. On that day he will stand on the Mount of Olives. It's east of Jerusalem. It will be split in two from east to west. Half of the mountain will move north. The other half will move south. A large valley will be formed. The people will run away through that mountain valley. It will reach all the way to Azel. They'll run away just as they ran from the earthquake when Uzziah was king of Judah. Then the LORD my God will come. All the holy ones will come with him.

There won't be any sunlight on that day. There will be no cold, frosty darkness either. It will be a day unlike any other. It will be a day known only to the LORD. It won't be separated into day and night. After that day is over, there will be light again.

At that time water that gives life will flow out from Jerusalem. Half of it will run east into the Dead Sea. The other half will go west to the Mediterranean Sea. The water will flow in summer and winter.

The LORD will be king over the whole earth. On that day there will be one LORD. His name will be the only name.

The whole land south of Jerusalem will be changed. From Geba to Rimmon it will become like the Arabah Valley. But Jerusalem will be raised up high. It will be raised from the Benjamin Gate to the First Gate to the Corner Gate. It will be raised from the Tower of Hananel to the royal winepresses. And it will remain in its place. People will live in it. Jerusalem will never be destroyed again. It will be secure.

The LORD will punish all the nations that fought against Jerusalem. He'll strike them with a plague. It will make their bodies rot while they are still standing on their feet. Their eyes will rot in their heads. Their tongues will rot in their mouths. On that day the LORD will fill people with great panic. They will grab one another by the hand. And they'll attack one another. Judah will also fight at Jerusalem. The wealth of all the surrounding nations will be collected. Huge amounts of gold, silver and clothes will be gathered up. The same kind of plague will strike the horses, mules, camels and donkeys. In fact, it will strike all the animals in the army camps.

But some people from all the nations that have attacked Jerusalem will still be left alive. All of them will go up there to worship the King. He is the LORD who rules over all. Year after year these people will celebrate the Feast of Booths. Some nations might not go up to Jerusalem to worship the King. If they don't, they won't have any rain. The people of Egypt might not go up there to take part. Then they won't have any rain either. That's the plague the LORD will send on the nations that don't go to celebrate the Feast of Booths. Egypt will be punished. So will all the other nations that don't celebrate the feast.

On that day "Holy to the LORD" will be carved on the bells of the horses. The cooking pots in the LORD's temple will be just like the sacred bowls in front of the altar for burnt offerings. Every pot in Jerusalem and Judah will be set apart to the LORD. All those who come to offer sacrifices will get some of the pots and cook in them. At that time there won't be any Canaanites in the LORD's temple. He is the LORD who rules over all.

remember what you read

1. What is something you noticed for the first time?

_____

_____

_____

_____

2. What questions did you have?

_____

_____

_____

_____

3. Was there anything that bothered you?

_____

_____

_____

_____

4. What did you learn about loving God?

_____

_____

_____

_____

5. What did you learn about loving others?

_____

_____

_____

_____

introduction to Joel

Joel doesn't give the name of a king he is prophesying to. It is hard to know when he spoke these words. It doesn't really matter too much, though. Joel is speaking the message of all the prophets. He uses phrases you might remember from other prophets. If there is suffering, God's people should be sure they are obeying him, and he will take care of them.

⌇⌇⌇

A message from the LORD came to Joel, the son of Pethuel. Here is what Joel said.

Elders, listen to me.
   Pay attention, all you who live in the land.
Has anything like this ever happened in your whole life?
   Did it ever happen to your people
   who lived long ago?
Tell your children about it.
   Let them tell their children.
And let their children tell it
   to those who live after them.
The giant locusts have eaten
   what the common locusts have left.
The young locusts have eaten
   what the giant locusts have left.
And other locusts have eaten
   what the young locusts have left.

No one brings grain offerings and drink offerings
   to the Lord's house anymore.
So the priests who serve the Lord
   are filled with sorrow.
Our fields are wiped out.
   The ground is dried up.
The grain is destroyed.
   The fresh wine is gone.
   And there isn't any more olive oil.
Farmers, be sad.
   Cry, you who grow vines.
Mourn because the wheat and barley are gone.
   The crops in the fields are destroyed.
The vines and fig trees are dried up.
   The pomegranate, palm and apple trees
   don't have any fruit on them.
In fact, all the trees in the fields are dried up.
   And my people's joy has faded away.

Priests, put on the clothing of sadness and mourn.
   Cry, you who serve at the altar.
Come, you who serve my God in the temple.
   Spend the night dressed in the clothes of sadness.
Weep because no one brings grain offerings and drink offerings
   to the house of your God anymore.
Announce a holy fast.
   Tell the people not to eat anything.
   Gather them together for a special service.
Send for the elders
   and all who live in the land.
Have them come to the house of the Lord your God.
   And pray to him.

The day of the Lord is near.
   How sad it will be on that day!
   The Mighty One is coming to destroy you.

Our food has been taken away
　　right in front of our eyes.
There isn't any joy or gladness
　　in the house of our God.
The seeds have dried up in the ground.
　　The grain is also gone.
The storerooms have been destroyed.
　　The barns are broken down.
Listen to the cattle groan!
　　The herds wander around.
They don't have any grass to eat.
　　The flocks of sheep are also suffering.

Priests, blow the trumpets in Zion.
　　Give a warning on my holy mountain.
Let everyone who lives in the land tremble with fear.
　　The day of the LORD is coming.
　　It is very near.
That day will be dark and sad.
　　It will be black and cloudy.
A huge army of locusts is coming.
　　They will spread across the mountains
　　like the sun when it rises.
There has never been an army like it.
　　And there will never be another
　　for all time to come.

Like fire they eat up everything in their path.
　　Behind them it looks as if flames have burned the land.
In front of them the land is like the Garden of Eden.
　　Behind them it is a dry and empty desert.
　　Nothing escapes them.
They look like horses.
　　Like war horses they charge ahead.
They sound like chariots as they leap over the mountaintops.
　　They crackle like fire burning up dry weeds.

They are like a mighty army
    that is ready for battle.

When people see them, they tremble with fear.
    All their faces turn pale.
The locusts charge ahead like warriors.
    They climb over walls like soldiers.
All of them march in line.
    They don't turn to the right or the left.
They don't bump into one another.
    Each of them marches straight ahead.
They charge through everything that tries to stop them.
    But they still stay in line.

As they march forward, the earth shakes.
    The heavens tremble as they approach.
The sun and moon grow dark.
    And the stars stop shining.
The Lord thunders with his mighty voice
    as he leads his army.
He has so many forces they can't even be counted.
    The army that obeys his commands is mighty.
The day of the Lord is great and terrifying.
    Who can live through it?

The Lord announces to his people,

"Return to me with all your heart.
    There is still time.
Do not eat any food.
    Weep and mourn."

Don't just tear your clothes to show how sad you are.
    Let your hearts be broken.
Return to the Lord your God.
    He is gracious
    He is tender and kind.

He is slow to get angry.
  He is full of love.
He won't bring his judgment.
  He won't destroy you.
Who knows? He might turn toward you
  and not bring his judgment.
  He might even give you his blessing.
Then you can bring grain offerings and drink offerings
  to the Lord your God.

Priests, blow the trumpets in Zion.
  Announce a holy fast.
Tell the people not to eat anything.
  Gather them together for a special service.
Bring them together.
  Set all of them apart to me.
Let the priests who serve the Lord weep.
  Let them cry between the temple porch and the altar.
Let them say, "Lord, spare your people.
  Don't let others make fun of them.
  Don't let the nations laugh at them.
Don't let them tease your people and say,
  'Where is their God?' "

⟳⟲

Then the Lord was concerned for his land.
  He took pity on his people.

He replied,

"I am sending you grain, olive oil and fresh wine.
  It will be enough to satisfy you completely.
I will never allow other nations
  to make fun of you again.

"I will drive far away from you
  the army that comes from the north.
I will send some of its forces
  into a dry and empty land.

Its eastern troops will drown in the Dead Sea.
    Its western troops will drown in the Mediterranean Sea.
    Their dead bodies will stink."

The LORD has done great things.
    Land of Judah, don't be afraid.
Be glad and full of joy.
    The LORD has done great things.
Wild animals, don't be afraid.
    The desert grasslands are turning green again.
The trees are bearing their fruit.
    The vines and fig trees are producing rich crops.
People of Zion, be glad.
    Be joyful because of what the LORD your God has done.
He has given you the right amount of rain in the fall.
That's because he is faithful.
    He has sent you plenty of showers.
He has sent fall and spring rains alike,
    just as he did before.
Your threshing floors will be covered with grain.
    Olive oil and fresh wine will spill over
    from the places where they are stored.

The LORD says,

"I sent a great army of locusts to attack you.
    They included common locusts, giant locusts,
    young locusts and other locusts.
I will make up for the years
    they ate your crops.
You will have plenty to eat.
    It will satisfy you completely.
Then you will praise me.
    I am the LORD your God.
I have done wonderful things for you.
    My people will never again be put to shame.
You will know that I am with you in Israel.
    I am the LORD your God.

There is no other God.
So my people will never again be put to shame.

✺

"After that, I will pour out my Spirit on all people.
Your sons and daughters will prophesy.
Your old men will have dreams.
Your young men will have visions.
In those days I will pour out my Spirit
on those who serve me, men and women alike.
I will show wonders in the heavens and on the earth.
There will be blood and fire and clouds of smoke.
The sun will become dark.
The moon will turn red like blood.
It will happen before the great and terrible day of the
Lord comes.
Everyone who calls out to me will be saved.
On Mount Zion and in Jerusalem
some of my people will be left alive.
I have chosen them.
That is what I have promised.

✺

"At that time I will bless Judah and Jerusalem
with great success again.
I will gather together all the nations.
I will bring them down to the Valley of Jehoshaphat.
There I will put them on trial.
I will judge them for what they have done
to my people Israel.
They scattered them among the nations.
They divided up my land among themselves.

Announce this among the nations.
Tell them to prepare for battle.

Nations, get your soldiers ready!
  Bring all your fighting men together
  and march out to attack.
Hammer your plows into swords.
  Hammer your pruning tools into spears.
Let anyone who is weak say,
  "I am strong!"
Come quickly, all you surrounding nations.
  Gather together in the Valley of Jehoshaphat.

Lord, send down your soldiers from heaven!

The Lord says,

"Stir up the nations into action!
  Let them march into the valley
  where I will judge them.
I will take my seat in court.
  I will judge all the surrounding nations.
My soldiers, swing your blades.
  The nations are ripe for harvest.
Come and stomp on them as if they were grapes.
  Crush them until the winepress of my anger is full.
Do it until the wine spills over
  from the places where it is stored.
  The nations have committed far too many sins!"

Huge numbers of soldiers are gathered in the valley
  where the Lord will hand down his sentence.
  The day of the Lord is near in that valley.
The sun and moon will become dark.
  The stars won't shine anymore.
The Lord will roar like a lion from Jerusalem.
  His voice will sound like thunder from Zion.
  The earth and the heavens will tremble.
But the Lord will keep the people of Israel safe.
  He will be a place of safety for them.

The Lord says,

"You will know that I am the Lord your God.
  I live in Zion.
  It is my holy mountain.
Jerusalem will be my holy city.
  People from other lands
  will never again attack it.

"At that time fresh wine will drip from the mountains.
  Milk will flow down from the hills.
  Water will run through all Judah's valleys.
A fountain will flow out of my temple.
  It will water the places where acacia trees grow.
But Egypt will be deserted.
  Edom will become a dry and empty desert.
They did terrible harm to the people of Judah.
  My people were not guilty of doing anything wrong.
  But Egypt and Edom spilled their blood anyway.
My people will live in Judah and Jerusalem forever.
  The land will be their home for all time to come.
Egypt and Edom have spilled my people's blood.
  Should I let them escape my judgment?
  No, I will not."

The Lord lives in Zion!

remember what you read

1. What is something you noticed for the first time?

_____

_____

_____

_____

2. What questions did you have?

_____

_____

_____

_____

3. Was there anything that bothered you?

_____

_____

_____

_____

4. What did you learn about loving God?

_____

_____

_____

_____

5. What did you learn about loving others?

_____

_____

_____

_____

THE LORD GOD

introduction to Malachi

God brought his people back from Babylon. With his help they rebuilt the temple and the city of Jerusalem. But within about 50 years, their worship in the temple made God angry. They hurt poor people. They were unfaithful to their families. They gave God sacrifices that showed they cared more about themselves than God. Malachi warns the priests and the people to truly worship God or he would destroy them again.

∾∾∾

This is a prophecy. It is the LORD's message to Israel through Malachi.

"Israel, I have loved you," says the LORD.

"But you ask, 'How have you loved us?'"

"Wasn't Esau Jacob's brother?" says the LORD. "But I chose Jacob instead of Esau. I have turned Esau's hill country into a dry and empty land. I left that land of Edom to the wild dogs in the desert."

∾∾∾

"A son honors his father. A slave honors his master. If I am a father, where is the honor I should have? If I am a master, where is the respect you should give me?" says the LORD who rules over all.

"You priests look down on me.

"But you ask, 'How have we looked down on you?'

"You sacrifice 'unclean' food on my altar.

"But you ask, 'How have we made you "unclean"?'

"You do it by looking down on my altar. You sacrifice blind animals to me. Isn't that wrong? You sacrifice disabled or sick animals. Isn't that wrong? Try offering them to your governor! Would he be pleased with you? Would he accept you?" says the LORD who rules over all.

"Now plead with God to be gracious to us! But as long as you give offerings like those, how can he accept you?" says the LORD.

"You might as well shut the temple doors! Then you would not light useless fires on my altar. I am not pleased with you," says the LORD. "I will not accept any of the offerings you bring. My name will be great among the nations. They will worship me from where the sun rises in the east to where it sets in the west. In every place, incense and pure offerings will be brought to me. That's because my name will be great among the nations," says the LORD.

"But you treat my name as if it were not holy. You say the LORD's altar is 'unclean.' And you look down on its food. You say, 'What a heavy load our work is!' And you turn up your nose. You act as if you hate working for me," says the LORD who rules over all.

"You bring animals that have been hurt. Or you bring disabled or sick animals. Then you dare to offer them to me as sacrifices! Should I accept them from you?" says the LORD. "Suppose you have a male sheep or goat that does not have any flaws. And you promise to offer it to me. But then you sacrifice an animal that has flaws. When you do that, you cheat me. And anyone who cheats me is under my curse. After all, I am a great king," says the LORD who rules over all. "The other nations have respect for my name. So why don't you respect it?

"Now I am giving this warning to you priests. Listen to it. Honor me with all your heart," says the LORD who rules over all. "If you do not, I will send a curse on you. I will turn your blessings into curses. In fact, I have already done that because you have not honored me with all your heart.

"My covenant promised Levi life and peace. So I gave them to him. I required him to respect me. And he had great respect for my name. True teaching came from his mouth. Nothing but the truth came from his lips. He walked with me in peace. He did what was right. He turned many people away from their sins.

"The lips of a priest should guard knowledge. After all, he is the messenger of the LORD who rules over all. And people seek instruction from his mouth. But you have turned away from the right path. Your teaching has caused many people to trip and fall. You have broken my covenant with Levi," says the LORD who rules over all. "So I have caused all the people to hate you. They have lost respect for you. You have not done what I told you to do. Instead, you have favored one person over another in matters of the law."

⚬⚬⚬

People of Judah, all of us have one Father. One God created us. So why do we break the covenant the LORD made with our people of long ago? We do this by being unfaithful to one another.

Here's something else you do. You flood the LORD's altar with your tears. You weep and cry because your offerings don't please him anymore. He doesn't accept them with pleasure from your hands. You ask, "Why?" It's because the LORD is holding you responsible. He watches how you treat the wife you married when you were young. You have been unfaithful to her. You did it even though she's your partner. You promised to stay married to her. And the LORD was a witness to it.

Hasn't the one God made the two of you one also? Both of you belong to him in body and spirit. And why has the one God made you one? Because he wants his children to be like him. So be careful. Don't be unfaithful to the wife you married when you were young.

"Suppose a man hates and divorces his wife," says the LORD God of Israel. "Then he is harming the one he should protect," says the LORD who rules over all.

So be careful. And don't be unfaithful.

⚬⚬⚬

You have worn out the LORD by what you keep saying.
"How have we worn him out?" you ask.

You have done it by saying, "All those who do evil things are good in the Lord's sight. And he is pleased with them." Or you ask, "Is God really fair?"

The Lord who rules over all says, "I will send my messenger. He will prepare my way for me. Then suddenly the Lord you are looking for will come to his temple. The messenger of the covenant will come. He is the one you long for."

And he will purify the Levites, just as gold and silver are purified with fire. Then these men will bring proper offerings to the Lord. And the offerings of Judah and Jerusalem will be acceptable to him. It will be as it was in days and years gone by.

"So I will come and put you on trial. I will be quick to bring charges against all of you," says the Lord who rules over all. "I will bring charges against you sinful people who do not have any respect for me. That includes those who practice evil magic. It includes those who commit adultery and those who tell lies in court. It includes those who cheat workers out of their pay. It includes those who treat widows badly. It also includes those who mistreat children whose fathers have died. And it includes those who take away the rights of outsiders in the courts.

"I am the Lord. I do not change. That is why I have not destroyed you members of Jacob's family. You have turned away from my rules. You have not obeyed them. You have lived that way ever since the days of your people of long ago. Return to me. Then I will return to you," says the Lord who rules over all.

"But you ask, 'How can we return?'

"Will a mere human being dare to steal from God? But you rob me!

"You ask, 'How are we robbing you?'

"By holding back your offerings. You also steal from me when you do not bring me a tenth of everything you produce. So you are under my curse. In fact, your whole nation is under my curse. That is because you are robbing me. Bring the entire tenth to the storerooms in my temple. Then there will be plenty of food. Test me this way," says the LORD. "Then you will see that I will throw open the windows of heaven. I will pour out so many blessings that you will not have enough room to store them. I will keep bugs from eating up your crops. And your grapes will not drop from the vines before they are ripe," says the LORD. "Then all the nations will call you blessed. Your land will be delightful," says the LORD who rules over all.

⟡

"You have spoken with pride against me," says the LORD.
"But you ask, 'What have we spoken against you?'
"You have said, 'It is useless to serve God. What do we gain by obeying his laws? And what do we get by pretending to be sad in front of the LORD? But now we call proud people blessed. Things go well with those who do what is evil. And God doesn't even punish those who test him.'"

⟡

Those who had respect for the LORD talked with one another. And the LORD heard them. A list of people and what they did was written in a book in front of him. It included the names of those who respected the LORD and honored him.

"The day is coming when I will judge," says the LORD who rules over all. "On that day they will be my special treasure. I will spare them just as a father loves and spares his son who serves him. Then once again you will see the difference between godly people and sinful people. And you will see the difference between those who serve me and those who do not.

"You can be sure the day of the LORD is coming. My anger will burn like a furnace. All those who are proud will be like straw. So will all those who do what is evil. The day that is coming will set them on fire," says the LORD who rules over all. "Not even a root or a branch will be left to them. But here is what will happen for you who have respect for me. The sun that brings life will rise. Its rays will bring healing to my people. You will go out and leap for joy like calves that have just been fed. Then you will stomp on sinful people. They will be like ashes under your feet. That will happen on the day I judge," says the LORD.

"Remember the law my servant Moses gave you. Remember the rules and laws I gave him at Mount Horeb. They were for the whole nation of Israel.

"I will send the prophet Elijah to you. He will come before the day of the LORD arrives. It will be a great and terrifying day. Elijah will bring peace between parents and their children. He will also bring peace between children and their parents. If that does not happen, I will come. And I will completely destroy the land."

remember what you read

1. What is something you noticed for the first time?

_____

_____

_____

_____

2. What questions did you have?

_____

_____

_____

_____

3. Was there anything that bothered you?

_____

_____

_____

_____

4. What did you learn about loving God?

_____

_____

_____

_____

5. What did you learn about loving others?

_____

_____

_____

_____

A Word About
The New International Reader's Version

Have You Ever Heard of the New International Version?

We call it the NIV. Many people read the NIV. In fact, more people read the NIV than any other English Bible. They like it because it's easy to read and understand.

And now we are happy to give you another Bible that's easy to read and understand. It's the New International Reader's Version. We call it the NIrV.

Who Will Enjoy Reading the New International Reader's Version?

People who are just starting to read will understand and enjoy the NIrV. Children will be able to read it and understand it. So will older people who are learning how to read. People who are reading the Bible for the first time will be able to enjoy reading the NIrV. So will people who have a hard time understanding what they read. And so will people who use English as their second language. We hope this Bible will be just right for you.

How Is the NIrV Different From the NIV?

The NIrV is based on the NIV. The NIV Committee on Bible Translation (CBT) didn't produce the NIrV. But a few of us who worked on the NIrV are members of CBT. We worked hard to make the NIrV possible. We used the words of the NIV when we could. When the words of the NIV were too long, we used shorter words. We tried to use words that are easy to understand. We also made the sentences of the NIV much shorter.

Why did we do all these things? Because we wanted to make the NIrV very easy to read and understand.

What Other Helps Does the NIrV Have?

We decided to give you a lot of other help too. For example, sometimes a verse is quoted from another place in the Bible. When it is, we tell you the Bible book, chapter and verse it comes from. We put that information right after the verse that quotes from another place.

We separated each chapter into shorter sections. We gave a title to almost every chapter. Sometimes we even gave a title to a section. We did these things to help you understand what the chapter or section is all about.

Another example of a helpful change has to do with the word "Selah" in the Psalms. What this Hebrew word means is still not clear. So, for now, this word is not helpful for readers. The NIV has moved the word to the bottom of the page. We have followed the NIV and removed this Hebrew word from the NIrV. Perhaps one day we will learn what this word means. But until then, the Psalms are easier to read and understand without it.

Sometimes the writers of the Bible used more than one name for the same person or place. For example, in the New Testament the Sea of Galilee is also called the Sea of Gennesaret. Sometimes it is also called the Sea of Tiberias. But in the NIrV we decided to call it the Sea of Galilee everywhere it appears. We called it that because that is its most familiar name.

We also wanted to help you learn the names of people and places in the Bible. So sometimes we provided names even in verses where those names don't actually appear. For example, sometimes the Bible says "the River" where it means "the Euphrates River." In those places, we used the full name "the Euphrates River." Sometimes the word "Pharaoh" in the Bible means "Pharaoh Hophra." In those places, we used his full name "Pharaoh Hophra." We did all these things in order to make the NIrV as clear as possible.

Does the NIrV Say What the First Writers of the Bible Said?

We wanted the NIrV to say just what the first writers of the Bible said. So we kept checking the Greek New Testament as we did our work. That's because the New Testament's first writers used Greek. We also kept checking the Hebrew Old Testament as we did our work. That's because the Old Testament's first writers used Hebrew.

We used the best copies of the Greek New Testament. We also used the best copies of the Hebrew Old Testament. Older English Bibles couldn't use those copies because they had not yet been found. The oldest copies are best because they are closer in time to the ones the first Bible writers wrote. That's why we kept checking the older copies instead of the newer ones.

Some newer copies of the Greek New Testament added several verses that the older ones don't have. Sometimes it's several verses in a row. This occurs at Mark 16:9–20 and John 7:53—8:11. We have included these verses in the NIrV. Sometimes the newer copies added only a single verse. An example is Mark 9:44. That verse is not in the oldest Greek New Testaments. So we put the verse number 43/44 right before Mark 9:43. You can look on the list below for Mark 9:44 and locate the verse that was added.

Verses That Were Not Found in Oldest Greek New Testaments

Matthew 17:21	But that kind does not go out except by prayer and fasting.
Matthew 18:11	The Son of Man came to save what was lost.
Matthew 23:14	How terrible for you, teachers of the law and Pharisees! You pretenders! You take over the houses of widows. You say long prayers to show off. So God will punish you much more.
Mark 7:16	Everyone who has ears to hear should listen.
Mark 9:44	In hell, / " 'the worms don't die, / and the fire doesn't go out.'
Mark 9:46	In hell, / " 'the worms don't die, / and the fire doesn't go out.'
Mark 11:26	But if you do not forgive, your Father who is in heaven will not forgive your sins either.
Mark 15:28	Scripture came true. It says, "And he was counted among those who disobey the law."
Luke 17:36	Two men will be in the field. One will be taken and the other left.
Luke 23:17	It was Pilate's duty to let one prisoner go free for them at the Feast.
John 5:4	From time to time an angel of the Lord would come down. The angel would stir up the waters. The first disabled person to go into the pool after it was stirred would be healed.
Acts 8:37	Philip said, "If you believe with all your heart, you can." The official answered, "I believe that Jesus Christ is the Son of God."
Acts 15:34	But Silas decided to remain there.
Acts 24:7	But Lysias, the commander, came. By using a lot of force, he took Paul from our hands.
Acts 28:29	After he said that, the Jews left. They were arguing strongly among themselves.
Romans 16:24	May the grace of our Lord Jesus Christ be with all of you. Amen.

What Is Our Prayer for You?

The Lord has blessed the New International Version in a wonderful way. He has used it to help millions of Bible readers. Many people have put their faith in Jesus after reading it. Many others have become stronger believers because they have read it.

We hope and pray that the New International Reader's Version will help you in the same way. If that happens, we will give God all the glory.

A Word About This Edition

This edition of the New International Reader's Version has been revised to include the changes of the New International Version. Over the years, many helpful changes have been made to the New International Version. Those changes were made because our understanding of the original writings is better. Those changes also include changes that have taken place in the English language. We wanted the New International Reader's Version to include those helpful changes as well. We wanted the New International Reader's Version to be as clear and correct as possible.

We want to thank the people who helped us prepare this new edition. They are Jeannine Brown from Bethel Seminary St. Paul, Yvonne Van Ee from Calvin College, Michael Williams from Calvin Theological Seminary, and Ron Youngblood from Bethel Seminary San Diego. We also want to thank the people at Biblica who encouraged and supported this work.

Kids, Read the Bible in a Whole New Way!

The Books of the Bible is a fresh way for kids to experience Scripture! Perfect for reading together as a family or church group, this 4-part Bible series removes chapter and verse numbers, headings, and special formatting. Now the Bible is easier to read, and reveals the story of God's great love for His people, as one narrative. Features the easy-to-read text of the New International Reader's Version (NIrV). Ages 8-12.

Look for all four books in *The Books of the Bible*:

Covenant History
Discover the Beginnings of God's People   9780310761303

The Prophets
Listen to God's Messengers Tell about Hope and Truth   9780310761358

The Writings
Learn from Stories, Poetry, and Songs   9780310761334

New Testament
Read the Story of Jesus, His Church, and His Return   9780310761310

My Bible Story Coloring Book
The Books of the Bible   9780310761068

The Books of the Bible Children's Curriculum
9780310086161

These engaging lessons are formatted around relatable Scripture references, memory verses, and Bible themes. This curriculum has everything you need for 32 complete lessons for preschool, early elementary, and later elementary classes.

Read and Engage with Scripture in a Whole New Way!

The Books of the Bible is a fresh yet ancient presentation of Scripture ideal for personal or small group use. This 4-part Bible removes chapter and verse numbers, headings, and special formatting so the Bible is easier to read. The Bible text featured is the accurate, readable, and clear New International Version.

To get the entire Bible, look for all four books in *The Books of the Bible*:

Covenant History
Discover the Origins of God's People   9780310448037

The Prophets
Listen to God's Messengers Proclaiming Hope and Truth   9780310448044

The Writings
Find Wisdom in Stories, Poetry, and Songs   9780310448051

New Testament
Enter the Story of Jesus' Church and His Return   9780310448020

The Books of the Bible Study Journal   9780310086055

The Books of the Bible Video Study

9780310086109

Join pastor Jeff Manion and teacher John Walton as they look at the context and purpose for each book of the Bible. Included are (32) 10-minute sessions that can be used with large or small groups.